PRAISE FOR *SHOW AND TELL*

Blues musicians describe how you need to have lived the blues to embody them, how music transforms suffering, and raises up freedom for yourself and your community. Linda Litteral does just that in this astonishing compendium of art and writing devoted to healing from incest and abuse.

Her ongoing search into the arts is a revelation of how drawing, painting, dance, pottery, installation, and performance (along with the individual's inner pursuit of them) can heal. Her creativity is amazing—brilliant, yet humble and collaborative. She is gentle and furious as she guides us inside and out to address taboo issues.

Having herself tried many healing modalities, Litteral reminds us there is no one fix for individual and societal abuse, trauma, rape, and incest. This is a hard, but essential, read because the acts perpetrated are heinous and ongoing in all places. If we are to weave any healing back into the mix, we must open our eyes and speak up collectively. Thank goodness for the insightful art she makes and shares to help us do so!

~Helen Redman, Artist

A clear-eyed examination of life and personal trauma, this book accompanies an artist creating a healing path that cuts directly through pain to build a fulfilling life of generosity and truth. Using her intuition and creativity in navigating and challenging the forces that often pull one towards suffering or despair, Litteral chooses a journey that eventually leads to developing a new language and a new creative purpose. With a spirit of openness and exploration, she manages to speak to and nurture the artist she has always been.

There are many important lessons for all of us in Litteral's self-revelatory journey. One of which is the power of listening to and accepting your own story and the transformative power that comes with pursuing and using your own voice.

~Lynn Susholtz, Artist, Gallery Owner: Art Produce

This book tells a story not only in words but images. The author shares her journey openly and honestly as she communicates the violence that began even before she had any words. As we witness her surviving a childhood of incest and isolation, an adolescence of hiding from others and herself, domestic violence in her first marriage, and at last finding the means to share and connect as an artist. As a psychotherapist who has seen all forms of injury and healing from violence, I am impressed with this work as she reaches out to other survivors of incest and domestic violence with a clear message of "you are not alone." The information is expressed directly with the words she uses but even more powerfully in the emotions experienced in her art. Her understanding that the source of violence was not only her grandfather but generations of her family and a broad culture of patriarchal misogyny is uniquely valuable. I recommend this book to all activists engaged in ending violence. That activism includes surviving and making change. A way of using art to teach and inform the journey of one survivor or for us all is shown in this book.

~Robert L Bray, PhD, LCSW, CTS, TFT-VT

SHOW AND TELL

Healing From Trauma Through Art

LINDA GAIL LITTERAL

EMPRESS

PUBLICATIONS

WWW.EMPRESSPUBLICATIONS.COM

ADVISEMENT

If you are a sexual abuse survivor, I do not want to trigger you. Be advised there is material in this book that could. Please be in a safe place when you read.

ACKNOWLEDGEMENTS

I would like to thank all the people who made this book possible. My family, my therapists, and my friends were all instrumental in giving me the space and encouragement that allowed me to write this book.

I would like to thank Lynn Sushultz for giving me the physical space to work in at Art Produce. Having that private studio was crucial to my ability to express myself with words. Nikki Dunnan for her support and encouragement during the body movement exercise. Space 4 Art San Diego for having a studio open at exactly the right time to allow me to finish the art for this book. Thank you to Justina Aura Nemoy, Kathy Nida, Lynn Susholtz, Dr. Robert Bray, Mary Counterman, and Jennifer Leigh Selig for their direct feedback from reading the book.

Thank you to Dr. Robert Bray for his enthusiasm and support during the difficulties of putting my life on paper. His Thought Field Therapy tapping exercises kept me going.

I am especially thankful for my colleagues in the Feminist Image Group (FIG) for their support of my art practice and my process in creating this book. Their encouragement and participation in all the projects we have worked on helped me to grow and heal as an artist and a person. Thank you to Anna Stump and Ted Meyers at Desert Dairy Artist Residency for their support.

Thank you from my heart, for my husband Lance Reynolds and his complete support during my difficult emotional reactions to exposing myself while writing this book. I am thankful for my daughter Tamora and her unconditional love and encouragement. Thank you to my brothers and their families for believing in me. And a special thank you to Mary Counterman, my niece, for her knowledge, encouragement, and editing abilities.

This book was written for all of you who have experienced any type of sexual abuse. I hope it helps.

TABLE OF CONTENTS

INTRODUCTION
WHY I WROTE THIS BOOK

In patriarchal society, as a woman doing art about sexual abuse, I have been discounted, held in derision, and ridiculed, just as other women have been for art they've done about difficult topics. As an incest and rape survivor, my work is held in particular contempt. I am not supposed to expose the acts that were committed against me—never to be spoken of and never to be revealed in art. In graduate school I was told repeatedly that "we do not do therapy here", discounting the worth of my art, and separating it from the academic realm. When confronted with the topic of my artistic explorations throughout my career, many gallery owners, collectors, and viewers would no longer be interested in work that visually attracted them in the first place, again showing how this topic is not acceptable in the art world.

I was sexually abused repeatedly by my maternal grandfather from age three to age eleven. He was in his fifties at the time of the abuse. He lived with us on and off during those years, and most of the abuse happened in our home. The abuse silenced me for many years; the result of the trauma kept me too afraid to speak. The consequences of speaking felt too dire.

On another level, it was just my life, the abuse was normal, and it was just how the world worked. People used me and I kept silent. I hid inside my head. Drugs and alcohol became my choice to silence the anger and self-hatred. As a child and a young adult, I lived my life suppressing powerful emotions and continued to push aside my sense of self, just as I had to during the abuse.

I was a viewer of life, rarely a participant, completely removed from what was going on around me. I would watch other girls giggling, screaming, and jumping around. They were free to allow their emotions to be exposed to the world as they reacted to it. I was amazed that they did that. It was foreign to me to allow anyone to see how I responded emotionally to the world. My physical reactions looked different from everyone else's, so I had to hide them along with the secret of my abuse. If I were to expose my emotions to anyone, I was sure I would be ridiculed and laughed at. I felt different, outside of reality.

I never did any drawing or art as a child. It terrified me. Maybe I knew I would reveal too much. Art is a communication of the hidden; I was afraid my experience would just come out and my secrets would be exposed. I unconsciously knew it would be dangerous. The closest I came to making art was creating mud sculptures that were monstrous looking; I destroyed them before anyone could see and never created any more. The emotions they evoked were so big that it felt like I would explode if I allowed them to surface. I remember looking at them with a keening in my head: *no, no, no, no, no*. I was four.

I made life choices that were not safe. At the time, they were necessary to keep me silent and safe. I married at eighteen to get out of the house. I did not see another way to escape. Nothing felt safe at that time. My husband then was verbally and physically abusive. It took me three years and becoming pregnant to figure out I could leave. To make a choice to leave was one of the hardest things I have ever done.[1]

It was a matter of taking the next step, doing what needed to be done to survive. I went on Aid for Dependent Children, where I was offered a class on drafting and design. I began working in the manufacturing engineering field. After four years of being divorced, my ex began to stalk me. I was driving to a friend's when he chased me and tried to run me off the road. The State Police office was near and I pulled in there with the driver behind me who witnessed it all. The police did not do anything, even with the corroborating witnesses. State Police pulled him over and took his word that he was my husband, and could not do anything. Remember: Divorced for four years. Husbands could do whatever they wanted to their wives (and exes) apparently. I kept taking the next step.

I moved to San Diego, illegally, as I took my daughter with me. I ended up in a Michigan court and had to pay to send my daughter home for visits with her dad. I married again in California, where I felt safe enough for the first time to expose my childhood sexual abuse. That was the beginning of my healing process. It went very slowly. I was hospitalized when I realized I was losing time, and then I was incorrectly diagnosed with multiple personality disorder. Misdiagnoses and the wrong drugs held me back from healing for some time.

I went back to school at the University of New Hampshire, where I did a class on alternative healing methods for childhood sexual abuse. They had a wonderful Women's

---

[1] Two resources for people in similar situations are RAINN (Rape, Abuse & Incest National Network) https://www.rainn.org/ 800.656.HOPE (4673), and the National Domestic Violence Hotline: https://www.thehotline.org. Internet usage can be monitored and is impossible to erase completely. If you're concerned your internet usage might be monitored, call them at 800.799.SAFE (7233).

Studies department that allowed me to design my own course of discovery. This was when my healing in earnest actually began. I had taken a ceramics class when we were transferred to Charleston, South Carolina (my second husband was in the Navy), and continued art classes at UNH when we transferred there. I found a therapist who focused on sexual abuse in his practice, and an art therapy group for incest survivors. The alternative methods I found during my research were helpful. I participated in a national art show called *The Healing Power of Art*. It was extraordinary to see so many people exposing their stories in such compelling ways. Standing in that exhibit space was the first time I ever felt like I was part of something rather than just a viewer. The sense of belonging I experienced was a turning point and propelled me to travel forward on my journey through art.

After two more years we transferred back to San Diego, where I continued my schooling. I was accepted into graduate school there, where I did my MFA (Master of Fine Arts) at San Diego State University. My thesis was called *show and tell*. I chose that title from excruciating memories of that process in class as a child. The purpose was to expose sexual abuse through art, giving a visual voice to the voiceless. The entire show was dedicated to exposing the damage done by sexual abuse to children. I was 48 when I graduated. It was a difficult journey. Some of the faculty questioned the legitimacy of my work; was it art or was it therapy? It was definitely art from my standpoint. I was doing therapy and it was not this creative process. Yet, it was in this process of exposure through art that I discovered that the creative process itself is therapeutic.

For the next ten years, I was a "freeway flier" adjunct faculty at several colleges and a university. I entered art shows around the world and worked on my art. I continued to do therapy and continued to heal. The healing process as I experienced it looked like a spiral: move forward on the spiral, around and around, fall back on the spiral, around and around, repeat, again and again. I did a certification course on "Art 4 Healing" and began to teach private classes on that subject. As the colleges cut adjunct faculty, I began to volunteer at the Las Colinas Detention Center, a women's correctional space. I developed a class called "Healing Trauma with Line" that has been a revelation to me, and hopefully, a help to the women I have had as students. The line of the spiral of healing is central to the process of teaching how to draw for me in these classes. Approximately 80% of the women incarcerated there have said they have been sexually abused at some point in their life.

I then began teaching at Richard J. Donovan Correctional Facility, a male space, under the auspices of Project Paint. I am very open about my abuse, and since my art is about that, I tell my students my story through my art. Several of the students there have told me that they had been sexually abused as children and had never told anyone else.

During these years of making, showing, and teaching art, I have come to the conclusion that we need to bring the stories of abuse to the world. While the individual is profoundly damaged, society is also damaged by the continuation of abuse. The patriarchal construct of silence abuses victims, especially women and children, and needs to stop. The "Me Too" movement is a beginning. Only by exposing rape, incest, and sexual abuse will there be change. Silence around these topics needs to be abolished for individuals and communities to heal and to change the way men, children, and women live together. The taboo of silence must be erased.

There are many symptoms and damages I have experienced as a result of childhood sexual abuse and incest: disassociation, depression, PTSD, panic attacks, self-harm, eating disorders, self-medicating, acting out, guilt, shame, disconnection, destructive behavior, numbing, self-imposed rules, physical problems, loss of identity, celibacy, promiscuous behavior, loss of innocence, feelings of isolation, etc. All of these behaviors are a result of damage done to the victim—in this case, me. These behaviors began as self-protection strategies to protect my psyche during the attacks on my body. The subconscious took over and removed my psyche from the sexual act. As time went by, the self-protection strategies became an attack on myself. They unconsciously kicked in whenever I was afraid or in an anxious situation. The self-protection strategies I had developed were no longer beneficial to me.

As a child I sat on the ceiling a lot, watching my grandfather use my body, a surreal and strange way to remember my childhood. As a result, I did not have physical awareness of parts of my body for a long time. I remember standing in front of a mirror, brushing my teeth and feeling the inside of my legs touch; it was startling. That was the first time I remember feeling that. I was 38. It was not that I did not feel pain; it was that I was not aware of my body in time. I would sit and read in an awkward position for a long time until the pain was so great, I had to move. I did not realize I was uncomfortable until my body arrived at a certain level of pain.

I had a hysterectomy at 29. Throughout my menstrual life, I had periods that lasted weeks. I bled heavily; I would be weak, pale, and anemic from loss of blood. One of my fallopian tubes had collapsed and attached to my intestine. Would this have happened if I had not been sexually abused? I do not know, but I wonder. Did my shame and self-blame attack my body and destroy my sexual organs? Statistics show that adults who have been sexually abused have more physical problems throughout their lives than those who have not been abused in this way.[2]

The way the justice system labels victims, the psychological labels that are attached to a victim by doctors, and the way language is used to blame the victim for their abuse are a continuation of the abuse itself. The person who commits the sexual attack needs to be at fault before society can heal and change. I find the definition of incest very benign. Look it up and see how you react to the definition. It does not explain the act with the damage that it causes and the lack of choice a child has. I find that the incest taboo is more a taboo about talking about it rather than the physical act itself. The way

---

[2] acog.org is one place you can learn how the trauma manifests in women over time.

society attacks the victim (making them at fault) shows that it is the act of exposing incest and rape, rather than the incest and rape itself, that is viewed as wrong.

From my own experiences, I will share many of the results of sexual abuse and making art in response, in an attempt to describe visually what it all feels and looks like from within. The words *silence, shame, guilt, trust, secrets, rage, flashbacks, isolation, dissociation, numbness, innocence, identity, control,* and *invisibility*—all of these live within a sexual-abuse survivor with their antonyms, their opposites, existing at the same time. It is a struggle within ourselves to make sense of all the ways we are damaged and decide how to negotiate with ourselves and be present in the world. A lot of these effects are unconscious; we are not even aware that they are working in the background and affecting the choices we make in our lives. I sometimes wonder what I would have been like, what I could have accomplished, if I had not been broken at such an early age and repeatedly for so long.

Every survivor's experience is unique. We all respond differently. From talking to many people over the years who have been sexually abused, I find that we develop our own survival mechanisms that work for us as individuals and that might not work for others. This is all constructed in a vacuum as a child, since we have no one to compare notes with. Our psyche takes over and figures it out. A lot of people do not survive at all.

This book will also be a visual exploration of all of the different ways that abuse has affected me over the years. If you are reading this and have not experienced sexual abuse, my wish is for you to find more understanding and compassion for those who have. If you are a victim of sexual abuse, these are opening conversations you can have with yourself about your own healing. My artwork will be presented in conjunction with and become a visual explanation of the effects of my abuse. By sharing my story, I hope you will feel connected to a community of people who have experienced what you have. I want you to know that you are not alone. I hope that the exposure of my journey will lighten yours.

Linda

LIST OF IMAGES

POEM

"DAMAGED"

Black Is where my mind goes

Silence Is where I live

Shame Is what I feel

I am invisible

Body Remembers better than I do

Powerlessness Is a way of being

Helplessness Is a way of feeling

Injured Child Is always screaming

Guilt Is in my bones

Trust Is hard

Identity Is a struggle to achieve

Scream to the world

Visual voice brings change

Heal

Image 0.1   Image 0.2   Image 0.3
One: what was lost   *One and a Half: what was lost*   *Two: what was lost*

These images are a representation of the feelings that were lost to the abuse. I tried to think about what positive words I would apply to the children I have interacted with to determine what words to use. Those words then make up the lines in the drawing. *One: what was lost* uses the words *curious, determined, gentle, playful, trusting, confident,* and *adventurous* in the lines. *One and a Half: what was lost,* has the words *innocent, fearless, bold, open, strong, decisive,* and *brave* making up the lines. *Two: what was lost,* is a compilation of the words *energetic, joyful, loving, focused, radiant, happy,* and *affectionate* making up the lines. They are images of me at those ages.

CHAPTER 1
BLACK SPACE: DISSOCIATION

Where do I hide? The blackness within is a place of peace, serenity, and terror. I found this place when I was a child. It protected and saved me from the world outside. When I had to escape, the doors would open and envelope me with safe-ness. If I were threatened and abused, I could run and hide in the darkness of my mind. Nothing could touch me; nothing could hurt me. The blackness was safe, a secure place that never changed. The abuse could not reach me there.

How did I find the darkness within? As a child, I was a victim of incest. My mind found a way to survive. Whenever Grandpa touched me, my psyche took over. My unconscious sent me to a dark and quiet place within myself that was safe and protected. I did not have to experience the pain and confusion that I was unable to endure. By protecting me then, dissociation allowed me to survive to adulthood, where I am now strong enough to look at the memories and recover.

I still do not understand the way dissociation works. Dissociation is a process of the mind that separates your "self" from your physical body. It is a survival mechanism that humans use in traumatic situations. Combat veterans, rape victims, or anyone who cannot survive whatever mental anguish their situation gives them, can experience dissociation. I have yet to find a doctor or psychiatrist who can fully explain how it works. I do know that it does work and it is powerful.

Separating from myself was automatic during the abuse I experienced as a child. As an adult, I began to dissociate in stressful or anxious, but not threatening, situations. I became aware of leaving consciousness and losing pieces of my life. I was going crazy. Maybe it had been happening all the time. It was so much a part of how I grew up, I couldn't see it. When the abuse was happening, it was natural. I didn't question it, just as I did not question the abuse. It was just what was. I could not have named it. As an adult, in my everyday life where there was no abuse, it was frightening. I saw myself in darkness, unaware of the world around me, going in and out of consciousness and never knowing why.

Confident I knew the material for a calculus test, the numbers would blur, and it was like reading Greek. As I stood in front of the board of the company I worked for to present a proposal I had conceived, I blanked out. In all these situations, I knew what I wanted to say or had most of the answers, but I became so nervous and scared that my unconscious would take over to "protect" me. What had been necessary to my survival as a child became terrifying as an adult. The helplessness tormented me. I became more and more withdrawn from the world and the people close to me. I was certain I could not think coherently. I made sure I was not in a position to have to perform: I quit working, stopped socializing, and decided to wait until I was "ready" to continue my classes.

I hid at home, leaving only to get necessities, and even doing that scared me. Getting groceries was a terrifying experience. I felt exposed and naked; people could see how crazy I was. If someone made eye contact with me, panic struck. My heart beat so hard, and I was dizzy; my chest was so tight, I knew it was going to explode. During this period, my current husband was without a vehicle and I would have to pick him up after work. It was agonizing to go inside where people could see me. I would call and ask him to wait for me outside. I didn't know what frightened me. I knew the people he worked with, but being sociable was more than I could do. As soon as this terror started, I would begin to dissociate, making it even worse. I was on a merry-go-round of fear with no way to get off or change the cycle of helplessness.

This pattern of fear was painful; hiding was my only alternative. I began to fantasize about not being in the world. It shocked me that my own brain betrayed me by giving up. I was afraid. I did not have control of my thoughts. What would happen if I lost control of my actions? I did not want to end my life. I began to change the spiral of pain. I went for professional help. As I look back, I am amazed that it took me so long. How was I able to stay sane as the black space ruled my thoughts? I did not think I was sane when I went into therapy. The effort it took to find and go to a therapist was tremendous. I did not trust anyone. I was exposed and helpless. The pain was stronger than me. I could not put words around what was happening. (It is still difficult to verbalize feelings.) My reactions were automatic and out of my conscious control. *Isn't everyone this way?* I wondered, but I could never have asked anyone if they experienced this phenomenon. I didn't think I was normal and didn't want anyone to know that.

With therapy, I started to understand the process I used to escape to my black space. I was trying to understand how my unconscious worked and develop conscious controls. As I learned to control my ability to escape inside, I could use it in a positive manner. I can now use my yearning for oblivion as a place to regroup and gather strength. With professional guidance, I learned how to dissociate when I wanted. I now have a say in what my brain does and how I want to live my life.

As I learned how to go to this place of darkness intentionally, I have had wondrous experiences. There is a process of creative imagination that guides me. As a child, I didn't even know I was there. I lost whole days, unaware they were gone. No one ever knew anything was wrong, so I was still able to function in some way. Now, I still cannot tell that time is passing when I go inside of myself. I can consciously go to this place inside me and come back when I am ready. One doctor explained it as being similar to out-of-body experiences that people spend their lives trying to perfect. Sometimes it is like that. I float to the ceiling and look down at what is happening. Usually, I become very quiet, as if there were nothing but darkness and peace. I can feel the rhythms of my body as they clamor for attention. I become smaller and smaller until I no longer exist in the real world. My mind goes black; the rhythm is quiet. No one can see me and there is no me in the outside world.

When I intentionally go to this mental place, I see vivid colors and feel a strong sense of peace. The colors are vibrant in their intensity. I feel the darkness around me, around the colors. It sounds like a contradiction. I am experiencing the colors of darkness. The colors are loud, shouting their strength, exploding in front of my mind's eye. I am the color and the darkness. I am strength and brightness. Colors float and swirl past my inner eye, soothing my whole being. I feel as if I am perfectly safe and nothing can hurt me. While I am inside, I know that everything is beautiful. I can experience pain and anger in freedom. As I soar within the force of darkness, I am free. The colors are alive, brighter than colors in the outside world. The intensity of color would be blinding to my physical eyes. I can explore and discover what I don't understand about myself. I keep moving within the colors, seeing what I can see. Once I was swimming. The water was warm and it felt alive. I swam down a channel of doors with bursts of color all around me. None of the doors opened; I didn't want to see what was behind them. As I descended into the darkness, fear and excitement intertwined. I can search for meaning in my black space of just experience. When I return to the physical me, I sense my strength and power. I am lifted to a higher level of awareness. I am centered within and sure of my place, solid and absolute.

As I learn about myself, I gain inner strength. In the colors, there can be images of strange things I don't understand. As a window into my past, it reveals a kaleidoscope of experience condensed and symbolized, flashing past my inner eye. As I write or talk about what I see, I discover lost memories, parts of myself I have missed, conscious memories too confusing to comprehend, separated into parts of faces and strange visions. Images float by to pantomime a feeling I can then recover.

Sometimes the blackness happens when I don't want it to. When this happens, it is a slower process. It develops as layers or levels of being out of tune with the outside world. As I become more aware of how it evolves, I can differentiate between the levels. As I begin to dissociate, darkness blossoms around the edges of my vision. I am so distracted that I cannot follow words that may be spoken to me. I see what is around me, and my hearing is drawn toward the inside. Sometimes words being spoken around me are garbled and don't make any sense. A secret internal scrambler turns on to garble the words. I don't know the code to decipher them. If I am reading, I cannot recognize the words. English looks wrong. It does not make any sense.

Some times are worse than others. If I am speaking, I cannot follow my train of thought. A sense of weight pushes on the back of my head. Thoughts disappear; a curtain of blackness descends to hide my mind from me. I will then stop and have to ask what I was talking about to be able to continue. Fear seems to drive this process; the deeper the anxiety, the faster I pass through the levels, and control slips from my hands.

It is not easy to confront my black space and expose it to myself. As I write, the edges of my consciousness become dark. My head aches as I try to look and remember the ways that dissociation affects me. My mind wanders. I have to take frequent breaks to be able to focus again. When I began to examine it with my therapist, the darkness was instant. Now as I explore it, I am so amazed at what I discover. I am driven to understand.

I feel like I am betraying myself by talking about this. By bringing it out in the open, I am exposing that inner place that was my best friend when I was little. The conflicting emotions that are awakened as I look into my psyche confuse me. It can be exhilarating and terrifying at the same time. All the emotions I experience there are overpowering.

The energy required for my inner search leaves me physically drained. I cannot look without paying a price. As my view of myself changes, I am left unbalanced. I am uncertain of where all this searching will lead me. It is hard not to chastise myself for being blind and afraid. Why is it so hard to understand myself? I can lose days at a time, feeling physically beaten and unable to do anything except vegetate. My mind runs rampant, never giving me a break from inner searching. The intense excitement and energy I experience when I dissociate leaves me drained. I am wrung out and left flapping in the breeze. I overload, doing frantic mental gymnastics. Processing thought is difficult, so I shut down. I wake up crying and am unable to stop for hours. Sometimes I have to keep moving, going so fast I cannot think, and other times I can't keep the thoughts at bay. I relive scenes of fear and horror, flashbacks of the past. My flashbacks rarely make sense and leave me helpless and hollow. The horror has no beginning and no end, aimlessly repeating images in my mind. Not having control leaves me frustrated and angry. I wander around knowing that I'm supposed to be doing something. What is it?

No matter the energy required, the inner explorations are illuminating, so I can't stop. If I could control them, I still wouldn't stop. I finally feel like I can begin to reclaim my life: past, present, and future. I need to keep going and experience the power of my mind, the wondrous and draining power that frightens and excites me.

Image 1.1 *Meditation #1: Mandala*

The artwork I made when I began this process of understanding my dissociation was dark. I was just learning how to meditate and I drew spirals of faces that developed into my personal meditation mandala. The first iteration was an ink drawing, which I was compelled to do over and over in black. After many years it evolved into very large paintings that imploded with color. The choice of colors for these paintings was very intuitive; I did not plan it. I would do a drawing of my profile and then start inserting tints and mixes of color. What felt right next to the first color choice? How did the shades all fit together? How can I make the image more vibrant and alive? There is a connection between the paintings and the intensity and brightness of the hues in my black space travels. Sometimes, I would go back to black and white, and the series evolved into triptychs: a spiral, a circle of color, and a circle of black and white, all composed of repeating faces. Me on my spiral journey of healing.

Image 1.2 *Meditation Wall*

My exploration, writing, and art around my black space began in 1990. I had just been in the hospital for losing time and was diagnosed with multiple personality disorder. I was in classes at the University of New Hampshire. Ever since then, I have been trying to understand, control, and heal the dissociation. It is also where I discovered that art is the most effective way to break down blocks in my psyche and expose more of my damaged self. Art making allows my intuition to lead—the images flow from my hand and body while my brain is quiet. My unconscious is often in charge. Words were the most difficult to use to describe or understand my trauma. The conventional therapeutic process was not very successful; it was just hard. It's not that I didn't make discoveries in therapy; it would just take weeks to get anywhere.

The creative process went around the blocks in my brain and came instead from my heart and my body. It was more descriptive and illuminative than any form of discovery about myself that I had tried. I am still learning things about myself by looking back at art I have made, seeing myself from a new vantage point in time and in the healing process. I cannot see all that is exposed until I am ready to accept it and heal. It is a difficult process; making art is another way to expose what should not be exposed. My internal and external worlds agree—it must be kept silent. It takes a lot of energy and determination to push past blocks that have been in place for years. The creative process heals and exposes what I need to see within myself to understand the damage, and it is worth the effort. When I do not understand the images that I make, there is a sense of knowing and strength in the process of expressing myself.

There is a sense of rightness when I paint these images. I feel like I am doing what needs to be done, and saying what needs to be said. The colors and faces allow me to see the pattern. The way it repeats and the way it changes. The way my healing goes is illustrated in these paintings. Some of the colors are distinct from each other, separate and alone. A lot of the shades are a mixture and blending of colors to become softer and more integrated. It is a dance around the spiral that I do in color and form.

The healing process around my dissociation is not complete, and after painting these images for thirty-two years, I still feel compelled to make more. I continue to paint them because I need to. Sometimes the paintings themselves dissociate. The faces disappear and the colors continue to circle and spiral in an abstract form, with marks repeated over and over in every color imaginable. I have not yet determined what this says to me. Is it actually a representation of all of my selves reconnecting and coming together rather than dissociation? I will continue to ponder and explore.

Image 1.3 *Spiral Meditation*

I also think that the viewer has an opportunity to heal when looking at art about sexual abuse. There is a visceral response to art that touches us deeply. That response exposes emotions we might need to look at and understand. I have had many people look at my work and begin crying, and not know why. As I talk to the viewer, I tell them what the work is about and why I make it. At this point, they might say, *I was sexually abused also.* We recognize what we see, and it affects how we see ourselves. This process of sharing is empowering within itself. We can see ourselves in others' work and know that we are real and not alone. A community appears; we are communal animals who need connections and an understanding of each other.

Dissociation is one of the results of incest, rape, and sexual abuse. It is common among survivors. It is also debilitating in our everyday lives. I need to heal this so I can live in the world, and not just on the edges. To participate we need to be present; dissociation does not allow being present. It seems to me that there are layers to this phenomenon, and as I heal, the levels shift and blend closer together. The more I can stay present in the world, the more I can experience it. As I heal, the dissociation becomes easier to manage and I stay in the moments of my life. If I am in a discussion that is uncomfortable, I can respond; I do not automatically run away in my head like I used to.

The process of trying to explain is empowering for me. Being able to write about this and stay present is a confirmation of my healing. I have tried many different healing modalities from alternative healing methods and more traditional Western medicine therapies. I find that, for me, making art is the strongest healing process, and it has been supported by every healing modality. Art was the doorway I needed to try other forms of healing processes. Without experiencing and working on them all, I could not write this. I have healed and am still healing; so can you.

The black space was the mechanism that allowed me to survive my childhood and consequently the experience that forced me to begin and then continue to heal.

CHAPTER 2

SILENCE

Silence is the most deafening sound of abuse. It is the sound of profound psychological pain. The need to be silent is real. It is another way to protect oneself from what is happening. The result is an absence of sound during an attack and even during questioning about abuse. Abusers often use physical pain, coercion, threats, and even the opposite, such as telling you that "you're special" or giving gifts, as ways to make their victims silent. Over time, if the abuse is repetitive, it grows into a way of life.

The process of writing this book is going against every feeling I have about silence. My body protests. I go home and sleep for long hours after writing for just a couple of hours. I have a low-grade heaviness in the back of my skull, the precursor of my black space. To experience this now, I have to consciously talk myself into the way back to this space and this time. I have been talking and making art about my abuse for over 30 years, and I still have the conditioned responses that I developed as a child to keep me silent.

When I was little, the need to keep silent was very real. If I hadn't, it would have meant the end of my life and my family's life. I knew if I ever said anything, the world would explode. I could not talk about it. If I even thought about saying anything, I would feel sick to my stomach. I would begin to shake. I would fall into my black space and later come back to the real world. The realization that my silence was my protection and the protection of my family came later.

When I was very young, three years old maybe, I drew or scribbled on the wall with my own shit. I remember my mom washing me in the sink and asking me what that was about. Why would I do that? She was upset. I only cried. I could not answer. Yet, was the drawing trying to communicate what I could not verbally? Memories of the earliest abuse are just confused. *What is he doing? Why is he doing that? It must be ok; he is Grandpa.* I did not understand and could not name what was happening. It just was.

I was mostly a silent child. I watched. I listened. I was the school dunce in first grade, as I could not speak when I was called upon. My teacher always pointed out to the class that I would not answer, so I must be stupid. It was a nullifying feeling; I was humiliated and felt as if I were an abomination. I ended up in speech therapy because when I did speak, my words were garbled and unclear. The terror of accidentally saying something I was not supposed to, especially about the abuse, made it impossible to speak at all. I was seen as slow, a problem. I sat in the corner a lot, the dunce's place. (My inner voice still calls me stupid, from that teacher's voice).

I do not remember being told to be silent; I just knew I had to. The world would explode if I said anything. I knew this. Since my abuse started when I was just beginning to speak, this makes sense to me now. Whatever way he encouraged me to be silent was completely successful; I do not remember what he did. The need to be silent grew and developed into a strategy for life. As a watcher, I saw how other people talked about their lives and experiences, and I tried to emulate their models. I must have been decent at pretending, as I made it through school, relationships, and work situations. I was just able to hide behind the act and get by.

It always felt like an act. I was never really present. I just acted like I was participating while staying hidden inside my body. I could see myself doing this, again as the viewer, not the participant, of my own life. I was not really a part of it; just my exterior body was present. Even after I was in therapy and wanted to expose the abuse, I still could not talk. I remember sitting in the therapist's office, silent for much of the time. Some therapists would fill the silence with talk about abuse and how it affects us. It did not really touch me. I was so far inside myself that I could not hear. Other therapists asked continual questions: "What did he do, how did that feel, what did you do?" I would not or could not answer. The questions felt like the abuse—they were pushing me, wanting me to do what I did not want to or could not do.

In one session, the therapist asked me if I could write about the abuse and then share that. I tried; all that came out were scribbles over and over until it tore the page. It looked like rage to me: dark, dense, and repetitive. It was a regression from beginning to write my name in real time to messy unidentifiable letters to using intense pressure to make jumbles of lines that just went on and on.

As the silence became a way of life, I could not speak up about other things. If someone bothered me because I was "slow," I could not tell anyone. If I was afraid, I could not tell anyone. I could not speak up for myself. If I was in an argument, I just listened to the person yelling at me; I did not respond.

In my first marriage, I could not defend myself. He was often verbally abusive, and occasionally it became physical. It felt like it was all my fault, a continuation of my early abuse. He called me names such as stupid, clumsy, fat, ugly, etc. I believed him at the time. I was certainly unaware of myself as a human being. I was only there for him to yell at, hit, and fuck. There was not much of me present in the world from 1973-1977.

After my divorce, I remember while coaching girls' high-school gymnastics that there was an adversarial attitude from the boys' coaches, because they thought they should be able to have the facilities whenever they wanted and push the girls to the side. This was in 1978. There was a schedule—as we began setting up in the gym for a meet with another school, we were required to give the other team a certain amount of time to warm up before the meet. The basketball coach, who knew the schedule, came over and started screaming at me that we couldn't have the gym because the boys were not finished. I didn't say anything to him; I just told the girls to keep putting up the equipment. He finally removed his team from the gym. The coach from the other school asked me how I could take that treatment without saying anything. I just shrugged. We ended the dispute when the parents of my athletes protested against that behavior to the principal, and he stepped in.

Silence did not serve me in that case and many others in my professional and personal life. It still is difficult for me to speak up. I very rarely defend myself with words. It is difficult to have a conversation that has the least amount of anxiety attached to it. I go silent. I stare into space; my automatic response is always silence. I have to push myself to participate, to keep going and to be present. I am a lot better at difficult conversations now than I have ever been. I have healed enough to stay present most of the time. One of the things I do is prepare for difficult conversations if I know I need to have them. This gives me more confidence in my speaking abilities.

Another result of the silence is that as a child I learned how to never remember any of my dreams. When I was very young, I remember waking up screaming from my dreams. They were always nightmares and they would repeat. There were two that would just go on and on. One was me in a tree in the yard, looking down at the grass. Any people that showed up in the dream would automatically get eaten by wolves. It would just keep going; I would see my family and friends being torn apart and eaten. I would gape, frozen in horror and fear, sitting on the tree limb. I would have this nightmare almost every night and wake up terrified. I would be afraid to leave the porch and walk across the lawn to get on the bus in the morning. The other dream was of a conveyor belt, although I could not have told you what that was then. On the conveyor belt were weird things—giant diamonds, human body parts, cars, staring heads bleeding on the belt, tools, rope, etc. They would just keep going by me as I was looking. I was frozen in place, somehow forced to watch. This dream also repeated over and over, night after night. I did not have any control over any of the actions taking place in the dreams.

I somehow trained myself in silence within that arena too. I was in kindergarten when I blocked all my dreams from my conscious mind. I would wake up and know that I had dreamed, but not remember a single thing about them. In the last two years or so, I have been remembering parts of dreams when I wake up. While they are always weird and unfathomable, it seems magical to me that I can see parts of them. The healing that I have done has begun to bring my dreams back to me.

When I was hospitalized for losing time, my mom and dad came to Maine to take care of my daughter. I was in the hospital for two weeks. When I came home, I had decided

I would tell my parents about my grandfather's sexual abuse. I was lucky; they believed me and supported me through the healing process. My mom cried and apologized for not keeping me safe, and my dad hopped right up and wanted to go kill him. My grandfather had died when I was in high school, so there was nowhere for my dad's anger to go. Mom also agreed to tell the rest of the family, my brothers and my cousins. Several of my cousins contacted me later and told me he had sexually abused them too; it was not just me. I was not alone.

That conversation with my parents was very difficult, and I was not sure I would get through it. It turned out to be a good thing. I think my parents came to know me better after that. I was able to be more present when I was with them. The conversations I had with my cousins were healing. Although sad, it was a relief to know I was not the only one, and yet it was also horrifying, a strange and uncomfortable place.

I do know many people from therapy groups who did not get the support of their families when they disclosed their abuse. Many were no longer welcome in their family for telling "lies." This was very sad and difficult for them, yet they all said it was freeing in many ways to no longer need to keep the secret and stay silent.

Another way I began to speak up at that time was in the first art show about sexual abuse in which I participated, *The Art of Healing,* curated and funded by Judy Wilbur-Albertson, CCSW. It was an international show about which she said, "This art is for the heart, for the mind, for the soul."[3] I volunteered as part of the process and had work in the show. Over three hundred artists participated. The realization that I could make art about my sexual abuse that could be shown to the world started here. I realized that others could see the work and also heal from it. Being part of this show was the permission I needed within myself that allowed me to begin my journey of making art about my life.

It is difficult to start new art around these topics. It is still dangerous to expose the abuse. My inner self screams at me to shut up. *What do you think you are doing? This is not safe.* It is always a process of fighting with myself to expose the abuse. It affects almost all my artmaking. What if I communicate the "wrong" thing? It is an ongoing struggle that has waned over the years, but is still there. I always reassure my younger self and try to make her understand that I am safe now and I can also keep her safe. She is still unconvinced that I am able to do that.

The *Storyteller* series was created around the idea of silence. They are clay sculptures I developed. The idea came from a trip to the Grand Canyon and the Navajo Storytellers that you see in the shops there. I was entranced by the idea of telling my story with clay and a storyteller is an important part of any culture.

---

[3] Robb, 1990

Image 2.1 *Storyteller #2*   Image 2.2 *Storyteller #2* Detail

In the early stages, they did not have a mouth. The top of the head was not there. There was just the jaw, torn away below the mouth, representing my inability to talk. The gold surface represents "silence is golden," one of society's tropes that keeps children silent. The throat on this first Storyteller has a house inside of it, representing home as the place that silenced me. What happened in the home blocked my ability to speak. Some of my Storytellers have eyes, ears, and mouths carved over the surface of the skin. These are open from the top and you can see inside the throat area where there are objects or carvings.

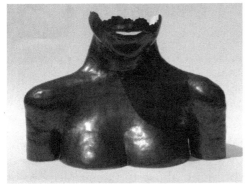

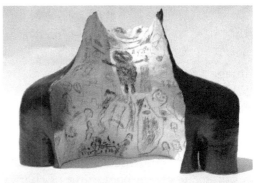

Image 2.3 *Storyteller #4*   Image 2.4. *Storyteller #4* Detail of back

The *Storyteller* series is evolving. They now have a mouth that can speak. Some of them have my face repeated on the interior of the body, which is open in the back, so you can see the interior body space. Each Storyteller is telling a different story. There are carvings, quotes, children's drawings of monsters, and flowers on the inside of some. Some expose the abuse, some expose the disassociation, and others show my black space or the nightmares. Some are showing the patriarchal constructs that allows the sexual abuse of women and children to continue. They are another platform that I am compelled to repeat. I must have many stories to tell, because I keep making them.

Another series of sculptures I have completed around the idea of silence are called *See, Hear, Speak*, addressing the cultural silence that surrounds sexual abuse. The forms have two eyes, an ear, and a mouth. Each part is just an appendage on the form. They do not make a face. They are urging you to use your senses to see and hear what is happening, then use your voice to expose abuse.

I highlighted the body parts that allow, sight, sound, and voice, the senses that are the most important to exposing and healing childhood sexual abuse. The texture is very rough. I used a stoneware that had a high amount of grog and then sponged away clay particles to expose it on the surface. It represents the feeling a survivor always has of rough internal emotions and internal responses, that someone looking at them would never see. It is not a smooth way of being.

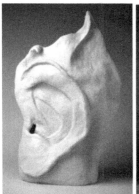 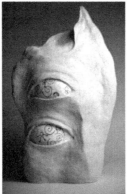  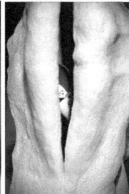

Image 2.5
See, Hear, Speak
Side One

Image 2.6
See, Hear, Speak
Side Two

Image 2.7
See, Hear, Speak
Side Three

Image 2.8
See, Hear, Speak
Detail

Silence is the underlying strength of sexual abuse because it keeps it hidden and allows it to continue. Silence defines the shadows where childhood sexual abuse exists in in our society. The beginning of change is bringing abuse to the surface out of the shadows and shining the light of knowledge onto the problem.

CHAPTER 3

SHAME AND BEING INVISIBLE

I have always felt shame around my responses to the abuse. I was certain it was all my fault when I was little. I made this happen. It was because of me that my grandfather used me sexually, and I did not even know what "sexually" was at the time. I am sure he enforced that idea. I remember statements like, "Look what you made me do," when he would touch me.

He would force me to look at ugly pictures of women and children naked and tied up, being used sexually. It was horrible. I would watch this going on from the ceiling. I was very small. He would hold my head so I could not look away and chastise me if I closed my eyes. I could feel myself getting smaller and smaller, disappearing from the world. He would lock me in the closet with the images as a punishment. I still cannot stand to be in small places.

The fact that my body responded with pleasure to some of the abuse also brings the feeling of shame. How could I like that? It was wrong; I knew it was wrong, but sometimes it felt good when he touched me. Other times, it was very painful. I would never know which was coming. It kept me in an area of sick anticipation: will it hurt, or will it feel good? I always knew it would happen again, just not when.

I always felt that I caused it. There was something wrong with me, so he picked me out of all the other kids. I must have been completely bad for this to be done to me. I had to be a horrible child for this to be happening. I must be ugly, mean, and just wrong. This was my punishment for being me. I felt broken, living outside myself. This understanding came later, after the abuse had been going on for a long time. Earlier, it was just what he did; it was normal and what I deserved.

What was wrong with me? What had I done for this to happen? Did I ask for this? I could not answer those questions, but somehow felt that there was something vile and ugly about me. I had done something horrible for this to happen; I had asked for it. I always knew that. There was a pervasive feeling of there being something amiss within me all the time.

These conflicting feelings were part of my need to be invisible. Fight or flight or freeze? All of those were present yet freeze was my dominant reaction. When I freeze, the feeling of invisibility rises. The shame amplified the feeling that there was something wrong with me. I had to hide the shame and all of the bad things about me. I was bad, so I could not be present with other people who were good. I was invisible, not only to everyone else, but also to myself. I was told what to feel. My true feelings were hidden and I was unable to form an identity. Who was I? Even I could not see. I had a sense of not being anywhere: physically present but not ever present in the moment. I was invisible to myself to be able to keep going. If I were to see myself clearly as a child, I would not have been able to comprehend it. The shame was all-inclusive, and it made me invisible to myself. If I were to see myself, my world would end.

I remember sitting in the living room on his lap. There was a blanket over us, and he had his hands in my pants. I was frozen in terror. My brothers were in the room watching TV. What if they saw what was happening?! I had turned into a rock on the outside with the emotions growing and expanding, swirling inside, until I felt I would explode if I moved. I can hardly watch cartoons anymore. They bring back that frozen me. I was so afraid someone would see, and I would be punished for being a bad, dirty girl. I would never see my brothers again. I would be sent away for what I was doing. I think I was four years old. Even now, I see a picture of *Marvin the Martian* and I freeze. The terror came from whether or not I would be exposed as the disgusting girl I knew I was. Everyone would know.

Another time, I was sitting at the kitchen table and he had his foot in my lap under the table. My mom was behind us making lunch. The sink was in the middle of the room and the table was on the other side of that half wall. The table was surrounded by three walls with just one end open to get into the bench and chairs around it. The fear of being seen brought up feelings of utter disgust and terror and made me so still and silent that I knew I was no longer there, invisible even to me. I had to be so still and prevent any attention from falling on me. I had to eat and look normal, while it felt like I would spew vomit everywhere. Within the stillness, I had to move my spoon, pick up my sandwich, chew, and not be seen. I do not have words for the utter nothingness that I was.

I wanted to scream. I wanted to run. I wanted to fight. I could not do any of that. I had to look normal. I had to be still and garner no attention. Remembering this and trying to be in those feelings is difficult yet important. I have to be able to explain for anyone to understand, to allow you, the reader, to get a glimmer of the forces that were fighting against each other inside me all the time. It was imperative that I stay invisible while I wanted to do anything else. To move away, to kick and scream, to fight back. I knew that if I moved and anyone saw, the world would end.

That frozen feeling invaded me at other times as I was growing up. I would be a quivering mass of emotions: chaos within while the exterior revealed nothing. Any sense of fear or danger and I would be right back there, frozen and unable to react. I was invisible, ashamed of being me. I was unable to allow any emotion to show through. The feelings were too big.

I tried to drown all of these feelings, when I became aware of them, in alcohol and drugs. In high school, I would escape through the chemicals, so I did not have to remember. It was a merry-go-round of highs and lows, a punishment for being me.

I was standing at the concession stand at one of the football games, talking to the girls who were working. They had heard I was going out with a guy from another school and were teasing me about it. That frozen feeling came over me; my heart beat so hard and fast, I thought it would jump out of my chest. I could see my shirt moving with the beats. I felt ashamed that I was interested in that boy. I thought they would see how dirty and awful I was. The feelings were overwhelming, and I had to hide them from everyone. I can remember watching myself laugh and responding to their teasing. At the same time, I was sure I would just physically explode all over everyone and had to hide the intensity of what was going on inside, frozen in space. I went and got drunk after that. Another way of being invisible to myself and others.

When I was married to my first husband, I felt like I deserved how he abused me. The shame of being me was representative of the way he treated me. He abused me emotionally and my shame made it feel valid in my mind. When he hit me, it felt like he was right.

Becoming a mother at 21 changed a lot of that. I did not quit self-medicating completely; I still had times when I drank or took drugs. I did not do them alone anymore, but in social settings, I needed to calm my fears and feelings of inadequacy. In 1989, I quit drugs and mostly just drank on New Year's Eve. I rarely have a drink anymore. I came to an internal understanding that I did not need those anymore. I was healing slowly and in stages. I didn't like the feeling of being out of control. I was lucky; I healed and stopped. Many women do not, and often end up in jail or dead from substance abuse.

I needed to understand who I was. Having a daughter made me realize I needed to give her safety. To do that I had to feel stronger and more in control. This was an intuitive, more thoughtful change of the way I looked at the world and me. Yet I knew I needed to change and understand myself to help her be who she could be. All of a sudden, I recognized I needed to be the adult.

Healing for me represents a choice. It is the ability to be in the moment and experience what is around me. To choose to stay in that moment and not be completely removed from my life. To have a decision on whether I move into my black space or not. To choose to be visible. To expose myself to the world and still feel safe. To recognize what I want and to move forward in full knowledge of what I need to do to realize that desire. Healing is living within my power and choosing to use it. I never thought I had a choice; I just took the next visible step and lived within the shame.

I did not like having my picture taken. It felt like the camera could see the truth. I was dirty. In pictures, other people would be able to see it too. As I look back at pictures, I can see the scared little girl in my eyes. I am still uncomfortable with pictures of myself. Shame makes it difficult to see myself clearly. While I understand in my head that none of it was my fault, there are still parts of me that feel that it was. I still freeze in tense situations. Thankfully, it doesn't happen very often anymore, and I move out of it quickly. I try to have a comforting conversation with my small child within and reassure her that it is safe now. I have the power to protect us.

I can still stand in the midst of a crowd and be alone. The feeling of being invisible can be overwhelming. It's as if I am everywhere in the room because I can see it all. Yet there is a sense from within of no one seeing me. No one approaches me; no one speaks to me. It's as if there is a force field around me that says *do not look, do not see,* and they do not. It is a stillness that holds me completely within its grasp. I am so ashamed of me that I need to be invisible.

Even if I am active in a conversation or moving my body, I have a sense of not being there, invisible to myself, unable to feel, blank. I am an automaton performing the tasks of living, not present inside. Only a skin, empty. This feeling is a total annihilation of who I am. It is me hidden from me. No way to feel what is really there, too dangerous. It's life-threatening to know and acknowledge what I am feeling. I hold my breath, barely conscious. My head directs; my feelings are dispatched to the deepest pit inside me that I cannot reach.

For a long time, I didn't do self-portraits. Looking at my physical self felt dangerous. I would not be invisible if I looked. While writing this book I have done several versions of self-portraits. It has been very difficult to look back at photographs of that time in my life when the abuse was happening. It brought up a lot of memories and feelings I try to avoid. I thought it was important to go there though, to release that fear of looking. To see what was, to move on to a future free from shame.

The one self-portrait I did in school was metaphorical. I created an installation that has a bowl or shard for each year of my life. Each year has a carving or an element that hints at memories. They are a progression from being broken, just shards, to coming off the wall and being whole. The bowls on the floor are beautiful. I will speak about this more in Chapter 9.

The self-portrait profile series is made up of the meditations repeated with my profile. They represent all of the masks I have had to wear, how pervasive those masks have been in my life, and how I had to hide my feelings and pretend to be present in the world. The colors are to show the healing and the extent of my self-understanding.

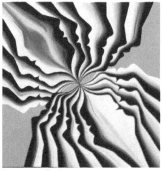  

Image 3.1   Image 3.2   Image 3.3
Meditation: Self Portrait #7 Meditation: Self Portrait #8 Meditation: Self Portrait #9

The black and white represent the dichotomy of my feelings: How I feel good about myself and hate myself at the same time. How the shame continues even though I know I am not at fault. That I know I am an artist, yet feel at times that I am not. This is apparently a common enough feeling for the psychiatric world to give it a name: imposter syndrome. For me, it's when I am present in the world, but feel invisible. The spiral represents the healing processes through which I have been traveling.

The meditation series (see image 1.2) paintings are an exercise in honoring all of my inner selves. Through color and the mixing of colors that are next to each other, I allow the good and the bad parts of me to be visible and in the world. This dichotomy of all the opposing forces within is balanced within the colors on the canvas. The feelings I have that are in opposition to each other about myself are represented. I hate myself; I love myself. I am terrified; I must keep going. I need to be silent; I have to speak. I am angry; I cannot show anger. I feel shame, while knowing I did nothing shameful. I think about all of these things while I am painting. My thoughts direct my intuition for choosing the colors that need to be mixed or next to each other.

I use complementary, analogous, and monochromatic mixtures of color. I use these combinations to represent the psychological morass that is within me. I try to bring harmony into myself with the colors I use. The process of choosing the colors and mixing them on the canvas is completely intuitive. I rarely plan the colors in advance. It is the color that feels right in that moment in relation to what has already been put on the canvas.

There is an understanding within me that says, colors heal. Use them. They can heal me and they can heal you.

Image 3.4 *Moments* detail   Image 3.5 *Moments* detail

Moments came about while I looked at and drew all of the photographs I could find of me when I was young and a few from adulthood. I built wooden house frames that represent the home as the place of abuse. I had to live there. I could not escape. The drawings of myself on the walls of the houses are in recognition of my survival of the trauma there. It was a difficult process. Looking at those images of me as a child brought it all back. I tried to feel what I felt then, to remember what it was like to live in that house, and to experience the sexual abuse. Then, I could put it in the past and not in the now. It was an exercise in remembering and knowing that I did the best I could then and could now leave it there, in the past where it belongs.

In drawing the photographs, I was honoring who I did not get to be, honoring that strong little girl who survived, and the innocence that I didn't get to experience. By doing the images I took back myself as a child and removed her from my grandfather's domination.

Image 3.6 *Moments*

The installation is kinetic in nature. The structures are all hung on swivels so if the air moves, the houses move. The houses can go around and the entire hanging apparatus with all of the houses on it can go around. This movement represents for me the ability to be visible, the chance to be seen, no longer invisible. The idea is that I can move now even if I could not then. It's an acknowledgment of that child, me, who is important enough to see.

All of my work is autobiographical in some way. The carvings that I call "possibility bowls" are a representation of my love of beauty and growing things. My long-standing need to grow flowers and experience them is revealed. I grew up in a rural area where my mom had several different flower gardens which were always colorful and changing in the summertime. I have always found them to be places I can stop and be, surrounded by the flowers. The bowls are a vessel to hold my dreams and desires. Ceramic bowls want to be touched and held. They call for our attention. The carved images are a form of armor on the surface of the clay and they create a safe place within the bowl. As you hold the bowl, you can visualize all of the dreams within—they are in the center of the bowl, representative of my center. It's a safe way to be present in the world outside of myself, within the bowl, yet visible. It's an intentional act of creating something that counters my invisibility, a piece of myself laid bare for others to interact with.

Image 3.7   *Possibility Bowl: Ode to the Rainforest #3*

This series of *Possibility Bowls* is my response to a trip to Ecuador. I came home with many images of plants from hikes in the rain forest. It is a magical place with diversity and beauty that is unmatched. I used porcelain and celadon glazes to capture the beauty I found there.

Making art is a way for me to counteract the feelings of shame and invisibility. Creativity allows me to fight back against the feeling of fault. It is a visual representation of my fight for finding me. My discovery of creativity and art making was the fuel that ignited my healing process. As I made art, my cloak of invisibility grew thinner and thinner. Now I can be seen. It was a conscious choice to expose my ideas, thoughts, and feelings to the world. It took hard work and dedication to achieve a sense of sharing them with you so that I could.

CHAPTER 4

THE BODY REMEMBERS AND HOLDS THE STORY

The continual numbing of my body protected it from feeling for a long time. If my body could feel, then the abuse was brought to the forefront of my mind where the emotions that I had blocked for so long could creep out. I always had the pictures of the sexual abuse in my head. The physical and emotional memories are harder to reach. Most of the time I erased the way it felt when it was happening. I had no emotional attachment or physical memory of those pictures. The abuse was just there: it did not hurt, I did not cry, I did not laugh.

The stillness of silence helped all of those emotions and physical feelings stay at a distance for a long time.

When I began to heal, or feel, my body began to remember. My flashbacks were mostly emotional and physical. I would be in a situation that was just normal and I would begin to feel extreme fear and terror. For no understandable reason, there would be an emotional flashback. I would be standing in line and not be able to move. Frozen in place. Another flashback. There was no reason I could see that would trigger these moments of abject remembering.

I would feel intense pain in my vaginal area for no reason. I would just be sitting at my desk and then I was doubled over and could barely breathe from the pain. What caused it? I don't know. There was nothing wrong. Or my heart would begin beating intensely as I was at my drafting table. Why? I don't know. It would happen at undetermined times and places for no visible reason: physical pain and intense fear.

The memories were crazy-making. I felt I was going insane. It was difficult to go out into the world, as I never knew what kind of reaction would pop up. People would look at me out of the corner of their eyes and move quietly away, if it lasted for very long. Or, if they knew me, they would keep asking me if I was alright; what was wrong? I couldn't tell them I didn't know the answer. I would guess it was pretty scary for them also, something outside of their normal understanding. Thankfully the flashbacks did not last a long time, so I would be able to get away from that space and that feeling. A lot of the time, no one would even notice there was anything wrong. I would just be still for a short amount of time and then keep doing whatever I had been doing before the intensity happened, pretending it was not there. I didn't know what was causing the flashbacks. Was it a noise, or a smell, or just the temperature of the air? I had no idea where they came from. I could feel very uncomfortable in a situation for no apparent reason. I would just be at work and feel like the walls were closing in and I would be unable to breathe. Nothing was going on that should cause that reaction. I was not being threatened in any way. I just felt unsafe.

For many years I always felt unsafe; it would just get bigger and harder to control at times. The world was not a safe place, whether in my own living room or in my place of business. I was unsafe within my body. There was an underlying understanding that something bad could happen at any moment. I could not have explained it to you at the time. It was just the way it was. I still get that feeling at odd times for no apparent reason. Something bad is going to happen and I am afraid.

My body was a war, happening at intense moments. Sometimes I tried to hide it with loose clothing, dark colors, nothing that would bring attention to me. At other times, I would wear what would garner the most attention: bright colors, cleavage showing, and short skirts. It has always been one or the other for extended periods: needing to hide or damning the torpedoes and throwing myself in front of the world, daring them to notice me and see.

I was always hyper-aware. I knew who was around me at all times. If someone was behind me or moving toward me, I felt them moving. It was like I had eyes in the back of my head or sensors throughout my body. You could not surprise me. People would try to startle me and I was always calm and controlled in my reaction. Friends would comment on my lack of startlement in any situation.

Was I really aware of everything around me or was it difficult to startle me? It's a good question. Did I just feel numb? Was I out of adrenaline? Did I use up all of it when I was a child? My reaction to intense situations was muted. I could see everything in slow motion.

I was with my first husband's sisters and their children at the lake one summer. One of the younger kids went out too deep and he couldn't swim. He was frantically trying to reach the surface. I remember jumping in and pulling him out while no one else even knew what was happening. My body responded as it needed to. I was calm and controlled throughout the entire event. Everyone else started screaming and carrying on as I brought him to the dock. Luckily, he was fine. Yet, my response was intense calm under pressure, while I would freeze and feel like danger was everywhere in the grocery line, unable to move. It was hard to be in any given moment. Yet it was easier to respond to actual danger. There was something to react to. My body knew what to do before I did.

Having sex with my partner was a quiet act of silence. It was difficult to feel intimacy during this time. I would need to go away during the process, just as I did as a child. I was not really part of the process. I just moved and acted as if I was. My body needed to be distanced from the feelings of touch. If any of my feelings came to awareness, I would freak out and jump out of the situation. It was not safe in my mind or body if I was able to feel what was going on. My whole safety system was set up to allow the sex to happen and not be aware of it within my body.

While I was aware of where my body was, I was not aware of what my body was feeling within those times. My awareness of pain or pleasure was dim and distant. Did it feel good? I didn't know. Did it hurt? Same thing. The contradiction of being aware and unaware at the same time is disconcerting.

Another physical manifestation of the abuse was my eating disorder. It began in high school in 1970 and was mild then; it later mutated and became more severe. While in Charleston, South Carolina in 1988, as I was beginning to think about seriously talking about the abuse and started art classes, a year of hell manifested. I would eat and eat and eat until I was in so much physical pain, I would have to purge all the food. It was a daily ritual. I lost a lot of weight. I went to the gym every day and worked my body to exhaustion. I looked like I was in very good shape. I was not. I would wake up in the middle of the night and exercise. It was one way to quiet the voices and feelings. I was not in control.

This process is and was a dehumanization of myself. I was destroying myself while trying to nurture myself. These opposing actions were tearing me apart at my deepest levels. Why do I nurture myself with food in a way that is dangerous and life-threatening? What does it accomplish for me? Where does it take me? The loss of self that comes with the sense of release is corroded with self-hatred and disgust. The numbness negates all of my humanness, both feelings and understanding.

I was trying to feed something within that was ravenous. There was never enough food to calm the need. For no reason I could determine, I somehow began to have some part of control over this process. I don't know how I was able to stop binging and purging. I occasionally have had bouts over the years since then. I still eat too much at times, but never to the extent I did then. Yet when I overeat, it is a mechanism of silencing my inner self, as my subconscious tells my body that I do not want to feel what is coming up inside. It is a frustrating and horrible feeling to be so out of control that I don't even know I am eating too much until I feel pain. There is an automatic reaction where the switch is pushed and it takes my consciousness out of the equation. I will start eating, then later come back to awareness and look at how much I ate and feel appalled. I am still trying to feed that ravenous self who needs so much.

This inability to know what I am doing in the moment is demoralizing in every way. To have a need so great that I have no control. To start eating and lose myself at the same time. I cannot describe what it is I need or why food is the mechanism that soothes me. During these times I am not present; I do not feel. There is some relief in not feeling, but at the same time, I am horrified by my behavior and feel totally out of control. The feeling is then an intense hatred of myself. I know I am worthless, less than human.

After I was hospitalized, as I wrote about earlier, I stood in front of the sink in the bathroom, brushing my teeth. I suddenly could feel the inside of my legs touching. I don't think I had ever felt that before. It was the recovery of a numb place; a physical feeling that was forgotten had returned. It was amazing and strange. How could I not have known what the inside of my thighs felt like rubbing together? They do that all the time. It was a discovery that I tried to think about in other parts of my body. Do I feel that? Do I ignore this? How much of my body is numb? How can I tell? The recovery of the awareness of my body in space and time began here. It was a slow and onerous process. I had to consciously choose to focus on it to have any success with feeling. I still have problems feeling my body in space. To be aware and feel my body at the same time is still not a natural occurrence for me.

I hold myself in one position for periods of time. I am not aware of enough of my body to realize I am in pain until it is excruciating. I might be drawing and my back will be almost to the point where it is stiffened into immobility. It hurts to straighten it and might cause cramps. I will be reading and become aware that I cannot feel my legs. They have fallen asleep and are so numbed that I have to move them with my hands to get the blood flowing again. This lack of awareness is scary. I would like to be able to feel my body so I don't have to experience pain to that degree. It feels like I am punishing myself.

The art is a representation of my search for self by trying to pay attention to my body. When a feeling comes up, it is usually associated with a place in my body. Fear shows through when my throat closes and I can barely breathe. When I cannot talk, my chest contracts and tightens. Stillness represents danger. It is difficult to stay within my body and pay attention. I keep trying.

Emotions and physical feelings still sometimes manifest at the wrong time. There is fear when there is nothing to fear, silence when there is no one to tell. I have to pay attention to myself and adjust my actions to meet the reality of a situation rather than my internal reactions. I am monitoring my body at all times to make sure I am reacting to now, not then.

One of the artworks I have done around the idea of the body remembering is called *My House*. They are figurative works that show the female form torn in half and turned around to face itself. The front of the body faces the back of the body, very close together but not touching. The interior of the body is exposed and has shelves throughout. There are objects placed on the shelves representing memories. They are everyday objects that have some meaning to me: a chair, a child's bed, a chicken, a fist, books, toys, etc. These memories are a search for the parts of my body that participated as a child, and the desire to know where my body remembers events from my childhood.

Image 4.1 *My House*   Image 4.2 *My House* detail Image 4.3 *My House* detail

These discoveries help me to remember in a safe way. It is outside of my physical body. I can look at the art and comprehend the past in a different way. By making art I am putting what I do remember into a new form. This allows me to analyze from a new perspective and understand from a new view. There is a healing component to that process.

Image 4.4 *My House* A series of 8

I have discovered a performance piece that uses my body to describe the thoughts in this book. Called *My Body in Time and Space,* Nikki Dunnan, a local choreographer and dancer, has helped me to define the movements of my body through space.[4] It is an intense process where we chose words or sentences from this text and assigned body reactions, or movements, to them. As I move through the space, I am reading my story physically to you.

This work is a very different process from how I usually work. Trying to match my physical reactions, such as asking myself where in my body do I feel a word, is personally transformative. Paying close attention to my physical reactions to a word helps me to discover from where my feelings grow. My body holds the entirety of my sixty-seven years of experience. Being able to bring some of that to the surface is cleansing and a way to nurture and understand my body. I chose words from the book to depict some of the ideas I have brought to your attention.

Nikki suggested walking in a circle and reading the words I am using. I was having a hard time remembering them and the movements that go with them. While I was reading them over and over, I began to feel tingles throughout my body. My hair stood on end. It was the first time the words felt like they were connected to me in a physical way. There was an intense feeling of rightness—I felt, this is what I should be doing now. I am ready to remember more. After this exercise, I was able to do the movements more smoothly. There was not as much lag time as I thought about what comes next. It flowed in a more natural way. My body was able to connect to my mind through movement.

As we worked, the process was extraordinary. When we developed movements to define chaos, it was the most bizarre feeling I have ever had. My hands felt as if they were moving in molasses or as if they were webbed and connected together. I could feel the world's energy surrounding my fingers and connecting every part of them together. Then the stillness within was achieved in a soft and creeping way. The stillness grew and grew as my breath slowed and became shallow. This is a different kind of stillness from that of the past. It is a stillness that I choose to go into. It is a mindful act to pay closer attention to what I am feeling.

As we talked about my body in time and space, we used some of my coping mechanisms to lead the improvisation of motion. Inside the back of my head where my black space originates would consciously lead the movements. Another space behind my head is where I have stationed myself throughout my life to watch the world so I could be outside my body—that's also where the movements were directed from. It was hard, and I had physical reactions when I tried. I felt dizziness, nausea, and blankness, and phrases would pop in my head, such as *hell no, I cannot do that*. Fear was in my head and throughout my body.

---

[4] The video of the process can be viewed at https://youtu.be/agwPWMZd1Kw

Being disabled makes the process harder. I have a fused ankle that does not bend, so it constrains the movements I wanted to make. Arthritis flares up as I work. It was an exercise in feeling what my body wants to do and figuring out whether it would be possible. I negotiated with my body to continue—I cannot do this, so I will do that. There was a new connection between me and my body.

There was a feeling of discovery and exposure that is gratifying. I began to feel parts of my body that I had never felt before. I let the body lead and expose the definition. Then I came back to the computer and tried to put words around the process. It was difficult yet satisfying in a new way. I learned about myself. Throughout my life, I have watched myself participate from a view behind and above my body. I did not experience it from within. I was separate and could not look at me. This process has helped to bring me back into my body so I can feel, see, and experience all together.

Image 4.5 *My Body: in time and space* video still

The Words Within the Movements a Connection is Discovered

Confront my black space
Expose it to myself
I acted, participating, hidden inside my body
Chaos within, exterior reveals nothing
Feeling my body in space and time

CHAPTER 5

POWERLESSNESS AND LEARNED HELPLESSNESS

For most of my life, I have felt a sense of powerlessness: an inability to move, to make a decision, or take control. As a child, I felt my life was completely out of my hands. Someone else decided when I was to be used sexually and when not. It made everything else immaterial. I would go to school, play with my brothers, eat a meal, yet how I felt about all of that was not important. The important thing was when would it happen next? How would I hide it? How would I keep silent? The uncertainty of what was going to happen and my total subjection to the sexual abuse controlled everything else. I had no control.

When I was little, there was a sense of unease all the time. It was unbearable not knowing what would happen or when. I never knew where I was supposed to be. I never knew what I was supposed to think or what was going to happen at any given moment. Even when my grandfather was not present, I knew I had to keep the secret. That overshadowed everything else. When he was present, the fear was more immediate; "What is he going to do? Is it going to hurt? Will someone find out?" It felt like I needed to hide, but there was nowhere to hide. I lived in a bubble of suspense and confusion all the time.

That uncertainty grew into a sense of impotence. "I cannot affect anything, so what kind of decision can I make? It does not matter what I want, so why want anything?" The feeling of helplessness was pervasive. It touched every part of what I was. The things I did decide as I grew older were reactions rather than decisions. Some of them ended up okay; others did not. Drinking and drugs to dull the feelings and reaction to pain—not healthy. Marriage as a means to relocate—a bad choice, as my feelings and I were still with me. I could not escape them. Yet in the position I was in, these were the only choices I could see at the time.

When I was a senior in high school, I learned about an intern program for the summer after graduation. It was with the National Park Service and it sounded very cool. I was unable to finish the questionnaire. It asked about things I could not answer. Who was I? What was important to me? What did I want to do as an adult? Where would I go to college? I had no way to write about these things. My family would not pay for college. I graduated with poor grades, so there were no scholarship opportunities. I was making $1.10 an hour, which was minimum wage at the time. I did not see any way to go to college on my own. I never even applied. The task of writing about myself was too much like telling. I could not write about me and consequently never tried. How could I write about myself when I could not see myself?

I was drinking a lot and hanging out with many people who encouraged dangerous behavior, such as indiscriminate sex or drugs, both in places that were unsafe. I met my first husband at this time, and soon after, we married and moved to Kalamazoo. His older brother lived there. He was a disabled Vietnam veteran and so we were able to buy a house. The drug and alcohol behavior continued. My husband began a campaign of separating me from my friends. His emotional and physical abuse was insidious, a slow buildup to violence. I felt trapped, with no way to change anything. He started dealing drugs. He began keeping stolen merchandise in the house. Strange and scary people came to the house. I could not affect what was happening. After a year of this, I was beginning to know I had to leave — I just didn't know how. Then I got pregnant and felt trapped even more. I didn't have any money. My job was minimum wage and part-time. It was not until my daughter was about six months old that I had to stop and think about the danger. I had to make a choice about staying in this dangerous atmosphere with a child. She was the reason I was able to leave. The job of keeping her safe was more important than anything else.

As I filed for divorce, the court made me move back in with my husband for two weeks: a trial conciliation. They felt it was better to keep the family together. I went back home before the time was up. He held a shotgun to my head and said he would kill me if I left. I felt he would kill me anyway. My daughter was in the next room. I called my mom the next day to pick me up when he was at work. I had a sense of impending disaster all the time. It was exhausting.

My only choice was to move home. It was actually a good choice. My daughter had my parents and loved it there. I worked as a waitress and then did a drafting program offered by the federal government for single parents. I was able to get a good job. Then three years later, my ex showed up and began following me around. He would show up at my workplace, chase me in my car, even sit outside my house all night. It was terrifying.

I was driving to a friend's house one evening and he began playing chicken with me. I was in my car and he was riding a motorcycle. It was near the State Police post, as I wrote about in the introduction, and when I was able to get past him, I went there. The man in the car behind me followed me and made a statement. The police did not even give my ex a ticket. They stopped him but nothing happened. I was unable to change anything that was happening. They said it was a family matter! We had been divorced for three years at this point. Even with a stranger saying he tried to hit me, it did not matter. There was no help from authorities. I was on my own.

The oil embargo of 1979 at this point was affecting the auto industry; the company for which I worked built equipment for the industry. I was laid off. This gave me the chance to leave Michigan. I had a cousin in the Navy in San Diego. He would let me stay with him until I found a place to live. Luckily, I found a good job before my unemployment ran out. Again, I was reacting to what was going on around me and making the only choices I thought I could. There was not a lot of planning or thought about consequences, just escape. It took the idea of dying to be able to make the move. What would happen to my daughter if I were no longer there? She would be given to her father.

As I think back about this time, there is a feeling of fear and hopelessness. I am on the edge of a panic attack. By exploring my feelings about the past, I am bringing them to life. I am slightly nauseated, my chest is tight, and the beginning of stillness is trying to stop me. The words are few and it is difficult to continue. At that time, I felt a sense of doom every minute. It was dark; where was I supposed to go? How could I escape from this man? I was scared. It was almost two years later that he found me again. He tried to get custody of my daughter; I had to go back to Michigan for the court case. I had unlawfully taken her out of state, since after the divorce she was a ward of the state. It was crazy.

In the end, the court ordered her to go to Michigan at Christmas and for two weeks in the summer to see her father. Luckily, his parents agreed that she could stay with them while she was visiting him. He was supposed to pay half of the plane tickets. He never did. When she was ten, I sent a letter to the court saying I would no longer send her to see her father as she did not want to go (she never had), and I felt she was now old enough to make the choice. He had never paid any child support either, so I felt I had some leverage if he took me back to court. I was always afraid while she was in his custody. He could have easily taken her somewhere and not sent her back.

I now need to honor the choices I did make, as they were the ones that brought me to where I am now. I suppressed all feelings as a child. That was necessary to survive. I did not tell; I could not tell. That, too, was necessary to survive. I did survive, so they ended up being the decisions that got me here. They were maybe not as bad as other decisions would have been. I think the act of leaving my first husband was the first step in my journey of discovering myself. It was a long and tumultuous road. There had to be tremendous pressure on me for a long time regarding this decision before I could actually make it.

The sense of helplessness I have been fighting my entire life comes from my grandfather training me as his sexual object. My fight-or-flight reaction was co-opted to stillness, complete and total stillness for survival. Now the trauma response has been expanded to be called fight, flight, freeze, or fawn. My amygdala was affected. It seems I no longer have a fight-or-flight response; instead, I have stillness when danger pertains to me. All the adrenaline flooding my body when danger is detected in any situation has nowhere to go. The stillness overrides any other response to perceived danger. I can respond to physical danger quickly. It's easy to respond to protect someone else in need.

I have responded to the world around me, rather than having an effect on it. In the past, I have rarely taken charge and changed the world around me. The next step was always about survival first and then moving forward.

It has been somewhat easier to make decisions in my professional life than in other areas. I can mull a personal problem for weeks before I come to a conclusion. In the past, after all that pondering, I would just do nothing. As a younger woman with a daughter to take care of, I could take action. What was the next step? Get a divorce, sign up for Aid for Dependent Children, get a job, get job training, find a better job, and so on. This was the logical progression of taking care of a child. I could take care of or fight for someone else, but not for myself.

I would hold my emotions silent within me. If there was a desire, it went by quietly. I did not have the capability to know what I personally wanted—instead, I would react to what others wanted of me. That was always easier than knowing what to do. I could not make choices, as I was not aware of what I was feeling. Did I want something? I didn't know. I was not able to allow any wants to come to the surface and be visible. Without knowing, how could I act?

My first thought was always to survive, when anyone asked me what I wanted; it was pretty basic. I could not verbalize a desire to be any more than that. "Did I want to succeed? What did I want to do?" was always the question, and I simply didn't know. The realization that I am in charge of me and my life has come slowly. I still have a hard time acknowledging that I can make a choice, that there might be more than one choice, or that what I might want is as important as what others want.

The more I healed, the easier it became to make decisions, to actually have a desire and act on it. I chose to go back to school and study art in 1990, but I only went part-time. I could not take the time for myself; it was not important enough. It took me seven years to make the decision that I wanted a degree and to earn my Master's in Fine Arts. I then started going full-time, allowing myself the importance of education.

After achieving my MFA, I would move forward in my career by being in art shows, sending my work all over the place to be seen. Then, I would not do anything for a while and fall back into that place of helplessness. Whenever I was successful, I would be overcome with the inability to move, to take that next step that would push my career in a direction where the work would be more visible. I have only been able to go so far.

Then I have to stop and be numb for a while before I can keep making the work that is important to me. I would have an idea and be unable to follow through and complete it. I would be distracted from my art by teaching. I was unable to tell anyone I didn't want to teach classes, even though it took me away from artmaking.

There is a strange listlessness that overcomes me and makes it difficult to move. It still happens at times. As I write this book, it seems to be showing up more and more. I spent this last weekend in my pajamas, reading all day. I didn't do anything else. That is not my normal behavior. I might choose to read, as this is one of my favorite things. This was different; I could not seem to do anything else. In the afternoons after I have been writing, I go home and read. Reading is also one of the mechanisms I have used to not be aware of what is going on within. I cannot seem to make myself go into the ceramic studio and follow through. I can barely make myself cook dinner. I am still; there is a sense of my not being there. I cannot remember what I read. I don't want to talk to my husband. I don't want to feel what is in the background trying to come forward.

This process of telling my story is beginning to feel more and more unsafe. I ask myself, why am I doing this? Why would anyone want to read it? What is the point of this? I have to make myself get up in the morning and go to the studio and write. I feel a power struggle within, between learned helplessness and my need to complete this project. In the past, a lot of projects fell to the powerlessness that overtakes me. I forget to do something until the deadline is past. I self-sabotage, things get lost, dates are forgotten, art is broken, I forget to call someone, etc. It seems to be self-fulfilling failure.

Over the years, this trend has gotten better. I do not go to that helpless place as automatically as I used to. I am in more control than I have ever been before. Yet, all of these things can sneak up on me and push me back to that overwhelming feeling of being unable to move. While the helplessness is still present, I am able to muscle through it to continue. I will complete this book and I will complete the artwork to accompany it. I keep repeating this to myself. My current mantra is that I will finish the book and the art. The fact that you're holding this book in your hands now is proof that I've succeeded.

I have used paper dolls in the past to talk about feelings of helplessness and lack of power. I did drawings of myself at different ages on cardboard to create the dolls. They were black and white, with no color. I then made clothing that had drawings and text on the surface: what was used to hide the past, images that represented the inability to move or to experience what was going on. I answered questions I have about myself in the text, exposing the sense of silence and powerlessness to the world. The clothing represents a shield and a way of exposing the past at the same time.

I used beads, ribbon, color, embroidery, and cloth to amplify a thought on the clothing or hats. I used different papers to represent the frailty or power of the feelings. Was it an ironclad shield that would allow nothing to penetrate, or was it a diaphanous feeling that floated around my body to keep me motionless? Dark and light, thick and thin, loud words and quiet words defined the place I was within my helplessness. Beads counted the distress. I disliked these works so much I just threw them away. I have no images to share of them. Another way of hiding.

I began a new series of paper dolls to use in a series of blown glass domes and ceramic bases. These were much smaller than the ones I made in the past. Some are outlines of me as a child and others are rocking horses. They are made from paper I have done different drawings on, then cut out in a series of figures that are connected to each other. They are then formed into a curving spiral of paper to fit under the glass.

The paper dolls are placed under hand-blown glass domes that I did. I took a class on glassblowing with Kathleen Mitchell, a local artist who has been teaching private lessons in San Diego. I did three sets of three domes in varying looks. There is one set that is clear glass and easy to see inside. The next one is an opalescent glass that is difficult to see through, and the last set is with a white-speckled surface that also impedes the view of the paper dolls. I then carved porcelain I threw on the wheel to make bases that the dolls would stand on with the domes nestled around the dolls on the base.

  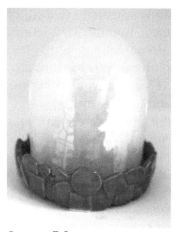

Image 5.1
Remembrance #1

Image 5.2
Remembrance #6

Image 5.3
Remembrance #9

Each series of three have different carvings. One is leaves which felt like a safe place when I was a child. The trees were where I hung out when I could and they felt like they understood my pain. The second series is the profile of a face repeated, the form I use on my mandalas for meditation and focus. And the third is made up of spheres, blocks, and triangles, the shapes that I played with to build structures as a child. Building blocks fascinated me as I stacked them up to make something else, then destroyed it and started over again.

While the dolls expose some of the feelings that were going on when I was abused, the domes make them hard to see. It is still difficult to look at the feelings from the past. The domes represent that inability to look at the past clearly or easily.

Yet the glass domes also denote an important thing, similar to protecting your gold medal. The glass gives the feelings a sense of reverence in that they were very important when they were happening during my childhood. As strange as I seemed to myself then, as I look back it is important to me to honor that little girl and the feelings she had. The glass domes represent my need to preserve those feelings that protected and saved me during that difficult period of my life.

CHAPTER 6

THE INJURED CHILD

I try to recognize the damage. The responses I have to triggers are so automatic that there is no conscious control. The subconscious drives my reactions; they happen without thought. The injured child overrides the adult.

It is still very hard for me to take into account my injured child self. I just assume she has learned what I have learned over time and healed. This is not accurate. When I have a strong response to something that should not have one, it is usually my inner child acting out and letting me know she feels unsafe. The separation between us is a definite space. There is me and there is the little me that is stuck in the past and always feels at risk.

It took me many years to recognize her, to differentiate between my response and hers. She is very strong. She keeps me safe when the world is not, even when I didn't know it. She jumps up and demands to be heard now. Yet, she is stuck in the past, in a place of uncertainty about when the abuse is going to happen and how bad it will be. She does not recognize that it is over 50 years since the abuse, that I am able to keep us safe now. Internal debates are common and I do not always prevail. When she is afraid, she makes me afraid also.

If this is just a construct, this placing of the fear outside of my adult self, it is very effective. She looks and feels like another entity inside me. She talks back. She demands attention. I have a visual of her. It is me at approximately three to four years old. She can talk. She reasons like someone older than that, but she can be childishly unreasonable. However, she is always afraid.

I remember a Christmas when we visited my dad's family. All of us children were playing with our new toys. As I watched the others, I wanted to participate. I felt odd and outside the group. They were cousins I rarely saw. I didn't know them very well. One of the others had received a rocking doll baby bed. I so wanted to play with it. When I did, the bottom came out and the dolls fell through. I was certain I had broken it, and this terrified me. I was unable to show anyone what had happened. I couldn't tell anyone. I hid in the closet until my mom found me. The board had just slipped off and it could be put right back in and was fine. My sense of being a bad girl overshadowed everything else. *I break things. I should not be able to play with them.* I remember waiting in the closet for someone to do something horrible to me. I don't have any idea what that might have been. It was just terrifying. I might have been five at the time; I'm not entirely sure. There is a picture of me sitting next to the doll I received at this event. It was taller than me. At this moment I remember feeling very scared and alone.

Grade school is a blur of fear. I do not have very many clear memories, just a sense of being afraid to talk, afraid to move. I remember being in a classroom and having the answer but being unable to voice it. I was perceived as different and strange because I had to go to special classes for speech therapy. I was always separate from the others. The speech therapist had a machine that made sounds that I was supposed to copy. It was difficult. I felt like everything I did was wrong. I hated and feared going to therapy sessions. The school I went to was one long building with classrooms on each side. Kindergarten and first and second grade were at one end. The speech therapist worked at the other end. I had to walk that long hallway of the higher-grade classes by myself, to and from the classroom. It was so long. It was always empty. It echoed my footsteps. There was a sense of danger all around me. I had to force myself to walk it every time. It looked like it grew and grew as I walked. It seemed to go forever. I felt very alone.

In different grades, I remember the teachers asking me if I was Leonard's (my older brother) sister. When I said yes there was always some surprise in their demeanor. He was the good student. I was not. This happened throughout my school years. I was always the one who was lacking, who had something wrong. It just emphasized the fact that I was broken. I was the injured child who wanted attention. It didn't even matter if it was good or bad attention.

As a teenager, I had to silence my inner child. I could not listen. It was too close. Drugs and alcohol were my answer to that. I was about twelve when I first had a drink. Wow, it made me numb. That was amazing. The memories were too strong. I was too close to them. They took over everything else. I could not function in the world and listen to the injured child and the memories at the same time.

I had to fight against the memories all the time. The pictures were always in my head. They were ugly. They made me ugly. After the abuse ended, the pictures seemed to get bigger. It ended when he moved out of our house when I was eleven.

The abuse was not the only thing he did with me. He taught me how to care for the pony he bought me, how to ride, how to trim and clean his hooves, and how to feed him and clean his stall. We would go for walks in the woods where he would show me the pheasant's eggs in their nest and teach me the names of the trees and plants. He took me fishing, ice skating, and roller skating. He taught me how to garden. It was all very confusing. I wanted to do all of those other things. I did not want him to touch me. It was not up to me. He did what he wanted.

He was still in my life after he left; the abuse just stopped. While it was a huge relief, it was also a big rejection that was hard to understand. The sick anticipation of when it might happen did not go away. I didn't know why it stopped, so I didn't know if it would begin again. He died when I was seventeen. As I walked into the funeral, I began to cry hysterically. I could not stop crying. I don't know if it was the loss of my grandfather or the knowledge that now it would never happen again. I was a mass of conflicting emotions that came out in gut-wrenching sobs. I was glad he was dead, and I was sad he was dead. He was the only one who knew what he had done to me. He knew me best. Then he was gone. My Uncle Billy was beside himself trying to calm me down. He walked me around outside, talking and patting my shoulder. We finally sat on a bench and he just let me cry. I missed most of the service because I could not calm down.

In my first marriage, my inner child accepted the marital abuse as normal and did not even have much of a reaction to it. It was all so much of the same feeling of being broken and useless. I had accepted that abuse as somehow deserved. After I escaped from the marriage and then escaped his stalking, the first person I ever exposed the abuse to was my second husband. I was 28 years old. That was a time of acceptance of myself. Something changed and I wanted to know myself better. I had my first therapy sessions then. They were sporadic and I never really addressed the abuse itself in the therapy. I just talked about current feelings and how strange they were. I think my injured child felt a little safer and allowed me to see more.

As we were transferred around the country by the Navy, I found and went to more therapists. I write about them in earlier chapters. The hospitalization, art therapy groups, and individual therapy were where I began to learn about my injured child, to see her and know how she had affected my reactions to the abuse. It has been a continuous journey to learn to listen to her and honor her strength during the abuse. I appreciate her ability to keep herself alive and to construct internal psychological protections that kept her functioning during the abuse. Playfulness was lost. I have always had a difficult time feeling a sense of openness and freedom. Joy is just a concept. I don't think I have ever felt it fully. I have brushed up against it at times.

Rage is so difficult to show: how it harms me, how it is damaging. My injured child may be calm on the outside, but inside is a raging inferno of fear, hate, and anger. This aspect of her is the hardest for me to look at and confront. I was never able to access this anger when I was younger. It was so big and overpowering. If I would begin to feel the anger, it would seem like the world was going to end. An explosion would occur in my center and destroy me and everything around me. Anger was the main emotion that was not allowed in our house.

She has held onto this rage and kept me safe from it my entire life. There is a fear in me that if I give in to the rage, I will just be a mindless mass of harm. If I show my anger, I will lose control and hurt someone. Anger was never acceptable in my childhood. I had no outlet other than physical movement to let it out into the world. I could punish myself with running, jumping, and climbing until I was too exhausted to move. I couldn't let the inferno loose.

Anger was always punished when I was a child. When I think about this, there is a vast empty place in myself. I don't remember what exactly happened. I just know I was punished if I showed anger. I was taught to silence it completely.

When I was in the sixth grade, I was sitting at the kitchen table doing homework one evening. My mom was doing the dishes and my dad came home drunk. He was yelling at her and then grabbed her by the neck and pushed her up against the wall with his fist raised. She had a small kitchen knife in her hand, and she told him, "Go ahead and hit me you son-of-a-bitch and see what happens." They never fought in front of us kids. I had never experienced this level of rage in my parents. This was terrifying in the extreme. Silence was always how we knew they were fighting. I sunk down in my chair and tried to be invisible. I didn't want them to notice me there. He let go of her and then went into the living room and passed out on the couch in front of the TV. We all were very careful not to make him notice us. While growing up, the thing that I remember the most about my dad was that when he was in the house, we had to be quiet. He was a truck driver then and was gone a lot. When he came home, he mostly slept until he left again. When I was a teenager, he got a new job working road construction, so he was around at night and silence was no longer as necessary.

There has always been both a sense of drudgery and intensity in my life, often at the same time. The drudgery is gray; there is no color or joy, yet I have to keep moving. I have to stay busy. I cannot stay still for too long, because then all the bad stuff jumps in and wants my attention. Although I have discovered work that I love, it sometimes demands that I push and push to not remember. It is difficult to stay in the moment and experience what is happening in the now, as the memories demand my vigilance. How do I keep them in the background so I can live in the moment? How do I honor my inner child when she wants to show me all the horrible memories and I don't want to look?

It is difficult to tell the difference between my inner voice, my inner injured child's voice, and the negative voices that have been programmed into me. All of these perceptions need to be looked at and contemplated. Then I can either go with the thought, or tell the thought that it is wrong, or tell it that it's a reaction from the past and has no place now. It can be exhausting trying to differentiate between the different perceptions to determine how and to what to respond.

While my injured child is always present, she is also very practiced at hiding. When I want to get her viewpoint, it is sometimes difficult to find her. There are deep dark holes within that she is adept at navigating. I can feel her moving around within, either trying to hide or trying to get my attention. Sometimes it feels like worms wiggling inside or a shiver of my heart or stomach. It can be disturbing. I need to stop and pay attention. Something is wrong or I need to pay attention to something else. I am still learning how to interact with and understand her needs.

I did a series of drawings from photographs of my mother. They are named for her age in each image. One is *Three*, the next is *Eleven*, and the last is *Seventeen*. I used her form and the words "Me Too" over and over to draw the image. There is a drawn frame around the image using the words "don't shut up." They are very powerful and beautiful. From a distance they look lacy and tender: the graphite material on a creamy delicate rice paper. When you get closer, you can see the words. Viewers have asked, "Is it embroidered?" There is a disconnect between the beauty of the drawing and the ugliness of the idea of the "Me Too" movement, especially associated with the image of a young girl. There is a sense of hope in the idea that we can now talk about sexual abuse without being silenced.

This was an emotional process. I found the images of my mom after she died. I had never seen them before. I used them because of the cyclical nature of sexual abuse in families. I would assume that my grandfather had been sexually abused, but I do not know. Mom and I had talked about whether she had been sexually abused as a child. She said she didn't remember and she didn't want to remember if she had been. I honored her wishes by not pushing her about it, but I was glad we were able to talk about it that much.

Image 6.1 *Three*

Image 6.2 *Nine*

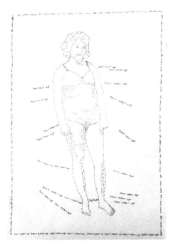
Image 6.3 *Seventeen*

I also created a house that is called *Chained by Childhood*. It is a wooden house-shaped frame that has knitted walls and roof. Chains were crocheted with chain stitch to hold ceramic faces that hang out of the bottom of the house. The house is suspended in the air, hanging from beaded strings at each corner of the house that meet and merge into one above the house. Because of the way the house hangs, when air moves in the space, motion happens, and it gently rotates in the air—a kinetic sculpture. For me, this motion represents the way that healing is achieved, by looking at the damage from childhood and seeing it transform or move from pain to acceptance. The strings used to hang the house have beads of black tourmaline for protection, rhodochrosite to heal sexual abuse, and rhodonite for healing emotional wounds from the past. This was a process of recognizing my injured child and letting her see that I am aware of her pain.

Building the house form reminded me that the home is where the majority of the damage was done. My grandfather sexually abused me in the house. I felt that there were no safe places there. I felt that my emotions and reactions were embedded into the space. I was left hanging in this unsafe place for many years

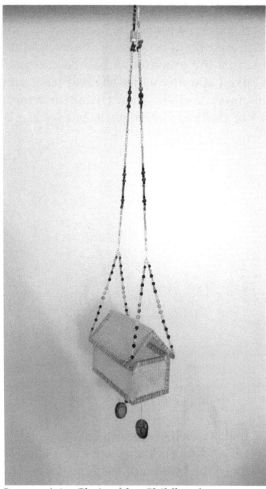

Image 6.4   *Chained by Childhood*

CHAPTER 7
GUILT

It is always my fault. It doesn't matter what it is. It is my fault. There has always been a feeling that if something is wrong, I had a hand in it somehow. This has been a pervasive part of my life. It made me want to make myself small and unidentifiable.

There is something about my being bad that makes everyone else good, until proven otherwise. There is an underlying belief that there is something wrong with me because my grandfather abused me and that makes me lesser than others, which means that I should be hurt. The expectation that I should be punished for what I did is always present. I participated. Whatever it was that I did to make him do what he did, his making it my fault was all too successful. How powerful I must have been to make this adult sexually abuse me over and over.

I remember staring at the buttons on the radio of my grandfather's Chevy Impala. The memory is still clear. The buttons look big and dangerous. They are scary. He has one hand in my pants while he drives, and my brothers are in the back seat. The bench seats make this easy for him as he made me sit right in the middle next to him. They are mad because they never get to sit in the front when we go somewhere with him. I am frozen, staring, and feeling guilty that they are angry. It is my fault that he wants me to sit in the front; I have somehow caused him to do this. I am bad. I have to hold very still so no one can see what is going on. He will do something horrible to my brothers if they find out. He has said so. I am a mass of swirling hate for myself, full of anger and fear. It is chaotic and black; there is tremendous pressure inside my body and it physically hurts. I may explode and hurt everyone. I have to stay very still and quiet, be as little as I can be.

I cannot even trust myself, as I was the instrument of my own abuse. What did I do to cause it? I know in my head that I did not, yet I was told that it was my fault. There is still that vestige of guilt that interferes with my seeing myself clearly. I feel that it is my fault at the same time that I know it is not. That strong tension can be exhausting to negotiate.

Memory has always been a problem. It was difficult to memorize things in school. The words would just melt away no matter how often I repeated them. If I had to get up in front of people to recite anything, it was always a disaster. I would flunk. My guilt would show through and be visible to the world. The feeling of guilt would overshadow any other feelings. On the other hand, I could pass tests without studying because I could remember what was said in class — tests were easier because no one could see me.

I remember some things very clearly and others not at all. It is a crazy quilt of memories from childhood. Some of the time is just gone. I don't remember anything. Other memories are crystal clear: mentally sitting on the ceiling of my grandfather's bedroom, watching him make me suck his dick while holding my head in place.

It has always been difficult to say no when someone asks me to do something for them. At work and at home, I would try to do everything and consequently exhaust myself. I would have to prove myself worthy over and over. I will do this for you so I can be seen as a good girl. I couldn't have a thought that was mine. I had to do what was asked of me.

In high school, I went to a basketball game with my older brother. He took off with friends during the game and I had to find a ride home after the game. When I got home, I was the one who was grounded for not waiting at school for him to bring me home. I didn't know when he would be back. I didn't want to stay there by myself; everyone was leaving. It was still my fault. There were definitely different rules for my brothers and me regarding behavior and punishment. Girls behaved a certain way, boys another.

When I feel anger, I know I am a bad girl. There is a sense that I am guilty of bad things if I get angry. The anger is my fault. The person I am angry with did not do anything to deserve it. I did. A sense of wrongness occurs within me if I get angry. In this moment, as I think about anger, my heart beats so hard that my head vibrates from the intensity. There is fear attached to looking at my anger. I am not supposed to be angry. Bad things happen when I am. I have no idea what those bad things are, but I know it to be true. And it is my fault.

As an adult, I can know that the things I wrote in the last paragraph are from my past and illogical. Yet the feelings are still there. I *know* I am not guilty of causing the abuse, but I *feel* that I am, even now, when my head says I did not. The feelings are a quagmire of guilt and I hate feeling them. I have to talk myself out of the guilt every time. I need to logically realize that I am feeling things from the past to be able to get past them in the moment. They surprise me when they pop up. They can cut my legs out from under me and stop me in my tracks, causing me to be unable to move forward until I deal with it all.

When I am angry, it is impossible to think. The guilt, the sense of being in the wrong gets in the way of everything. My thinking apparatus disengages and all I am is a roiling ball of chaotic feeling. Words do not exist. Response is unattainable. Anger is dangerous.

The guilt distorts my thoughts about myself. I always focus on the things I do wrong or the times when I'm not successful. It is difficult to acknowledge the achievements I have made, the positive work that I do. I am guilty of being a dirty girl, so how could anything be enough to make up for that? If I had been perfect instead of dirty, maybe the abuse would not have happened. It is difficult to speak up about anything. Someone will see how guilty I am of causing my own abuse. I am to blame for the pain I feel. I caused it.

I realize these feelings are false and a result of the abuse, yet, they ran my life and the way I navigated through it for a long time. I believed in my own guilt. It is still an exercise to recognize and negate these feelings of guilt. They can still pop up and affect my thought processes and decision-making. I have to keep telling myself that these feelings are attached to the abuse and not what I think about myself now. I am repeating this here because I need to keep repeating it to myself. I re-word it, looking at it from a different perspective, as feelings repeat themselves over and over. Perhaps it will stop. Perhaps it will sink in if I keep saying it in different ways: I am not guilty of my own abuse.

I did not tell—that makes me complicit in the abuse. I did not run screaming, so I participated. I did not say no. There are so many things I beat myself up about, especially for not saving myself. As I think about this, I know that the thoughts are absurd. I was three when it began. How could I say no? He was in charge. How could I save myself from his authority? I didn't understand what was going on. I didn't even know what to call what he was doing. So why do I still feel this tremendous amount of guilt? The pervasive and physical manifestation of the guilt is embedded in my body's cells, in my memories, and in my feelings. Understanding and knowing that this is wrong is part of the work I do to heal. I have to come to recognize that I am not at fault for any of it in order to recover part of myself. When my first thought is not about being guilty, I know I have done this.

The patriarchal mindset of the culture I grew up in—that boys will be boys and women are to be used—reinforces my feelings of guilt over the abuse. This idea is insidious and everywhere. It is in the way that words are used: It is the mother's fault that her children acted up. (What is the father's role?) It is in the way that products are sold: If you do not put these products on your face or body, you are ugly, and guilty of not being attractive to men. (Oh, the horror!) She was seductive, so of course I had to rape her. She wore that low-cut blouse and short skirt, so that gave me permission to yell obscenities at her, and on and on. The guilt of women and girls is one of the mechanisms that allows the patriarchy to exist. As women and girls, we are so exhausted from trying to stay safe that we have a difficult time finding the energy to change anything. Add the guilt from our abuse and it is even harder.

There is a level of anxiety that is always present. It is the feeling that I'm not doing it right, I do not know enough, I do not have the necessary level of skill, or that someone will see in my work that I cannot do it correctly. Nothing is good enough and people will see inadequacy in what I do. I don't have the right words. I don't have the best form or color for the art. The persistence of this tension within can cause me to give up. There is always fear that I cannot complete what I start, or that it will be really awful and will not express my ideas. I have to constantly fight against these embedded feelings of apprehension.

When I read that last paragraph, I realize in my head that it is ridiculous. I had a successful career in engineering. I have successfully completed many projects, ideas, and artworks. I am writing this book. I am known for my art. I am a skillful ceramicist. I have curated successful art shows. Yet that anxiety is always present in my body and my feelings. I have to push it back and ignore it to get things done. I have to talk to that voice that says I am unable, and reword the ideas presented in my thoughts. I know in my head that I am competent; in my body, I feel guilt and helplessness. I can act confidently, but I do not always feel it.

Unless you are a sociopath, I think everyone has some level of the feelings I have: fear, helplessness, anxiety, guilt, and all the others I'm writing about. I think that sexual abuse amplifies and expands them into immovable objects that are always present. As I try to do things, my feelings negate so much of my capability that it can be impossible to move forward. The process of pushing back and healing these is constant. If I let the pressure drop, I collapse, and I do that repeatedly throughout my days. A three-hour nap happens after writing for an hour. An eight-hour stretch of reading a fantasy book occurs when I cannot keep going. Sometimes I eat way too much. These are distractions that temporarily keep the feelings at bay.

I will say that it is much easier now to ignore the guilt and anxiety and to stay focused on my tasks. The feelings pop up strongly only some of the time, and they are easier to push back. Many years of trying to heal and understand myself are paying off. I could not have written this book five years ago. I have been thinking about doing it for twenty years. Until now, I didn't have the strength and conviction of who I am separate from the abuse to be able to say it.

It is still difficult to be mindful in the moment, to experience the now. The vestiges of the negative feelings are always present. Yet it is getting better. Meditation exercises are more successful. I can stay focused for longer periods of time. It is easier to be doing rather than just experiencing. If I am making something, accomplishing a task, or cleaning the house, I don't have to feel what's in the background. If I try to sit at the beach and just listen to the waves, I get uncomfortable. I have to move, to draw in the sand, to splash in the eddies, to be in the moment and not the past.

I made a mold of my face. I used that mold to shrink my face by slip-casting it, firing to shrink it and making another mold of that and doing it again. It took five molds to get to the size I wanted the faces to be.

Image 7.1 *Evocations*, detail

I then did children's drawings on the interior of the faces, the back side. There are fun images—monsters, families, houses, sexual scenes, etc. Some are in color. Some are in black and white. I used underglaze pencils, underglaze chalk, and underglaze liquid that I use for painting in color. For the faces themselves, I used metallic glazes. The glaze is like another mask; you cannot see the emotions or thoughts behind them. The face is still. There are 228 faces that have been hung on jewelry wire on a pole to make a wall of faces. The clays I used are all different skin tones. It is hiding what happened on one side and trying to expose it on the other.

The reflective surface of the metallic glazes also invite you into the work. There can be a mirrored image of you on the surface of the faces. This reflection is a representation of the many people who have also been abused. I invite them and you to be a part of the beauty of the art and the healing. The reflective surface also puts you, the viewer as part of the work, your face reflected on the surface of mine. We are all affected by sexual abuse whether we know it or not.

Image 7.2 *Evocations*

It was a difficult project in that I had to look at my face over and over. Even though the faces are the adult me, they convey the guilt by hiding what is within. There was emotional feedback that came from doing childish drawings of an adult sexually abusing a child. The children's drawings would draw me back to that place of guilt and fear. It is a repetition of my face that mirrors the longevity of the abuse. It would happen again and again, just as the faces repeat themselves.

Image 7.3 *Evocations,* detail of the back

CHAPTER 8

TRUST

I do not trust and I trust everyone. It is a strange thing to experience. The programming that I received as a victim leaves me unable to share or be too open. At times the opposites within render me mute and unwilling to interact. On the surface, I trust that everyone will not hurt me. When they do, I am surprised. On the other hand, the injured child does not trust anyone who comes near. Everyone is suspect and I expect them to hurt me. My interactions with others are fraught with the push and pull of those opposites within me. Should I stay and learn more, or should I run away? It is always a struggle. This dichotomy keeps me in an uneasy place that has always made it difficult to listen to my intuition about people.

I lived behind a series of masks that allowed me to keep my secrets. The situation determined the mask I showed to the world. As a child, I did not allow anyone to get too close to me. While I participated with other children, I did not let anyone see me. I had to be especially careful to hide around adults. I had to stay inside to be safe and I could not let myself out. It was too dangerous. If anyone saw the real me, it would be catastrophic. I did not trust anyone to see me. Then they would know what was happening to me. I knew if I shared what was happening, the world as I understood it would end.

Even now, I do not trust myself. I do not trust my feelings and my reactions. Are they my current feelings or are they the feelings I have embedded into my body and my memories? Am I reacting as is appropriate in a given situation, or am I reacting with my pain-filled, angry, broken self? Is it a flashback? Have I just been triggered and do not realize it? I question myself all the time about my reactions. Is this how I want to react to this situation? I question how I feel. Do I really know? A lot of the time it feels like I do not. I react to a situation now with time-honored protective actions developed by my childhood experiences. I have to think about the reality of now to determine how the adult me may be feeling and thinking about a situation.

In high school, we had grassers. These were where a bunch of students would go out into the woods with a keg and music to party. I was raped at one of them in 1972. I never told anyone; I just stayed away from the guy after that. I was pretty drunk and I am sure he thought I was participating. I was not; I was just unable to say no or fight back. It makes it hard to trust the people around you when this happens. Sometimes, local sheriffs would show up. They never arrested anyone; they just hung out and flirted with all the drunk girls. I don't know of anyone who went with them for sex, but that's what it felt like their presence was about. It was hard to trust the authority figures around me when this was the behavior they presented. This added to my unease—I should trust authority figures, I did not trust authority figures. It mirrored my experience and understanding as a sexually abused child.

From 1969-1973, we also had three different male teachers who were on the lookout for girls who would have sex with them. If you wore a short skirt to class, you could get a better grade. They would give girls rides after school, and it was obvious to me what they wanted. I would take the ride, but not the sex. Luckily, they were not violent and did not use physical force on anyone that I know of. Again, it was hard to have any trust or respect in the authority figures around me. It was just the way it was. Men wanted sex and they didn't seem to care if it was jailbait or not. They acted as if they could do whatever they wanted. I heard a few years later a friend told me that one of those teachers was fired for having sexual relations with a student. That was a good day.

So often my reactions to the world are old ones. To get to my adult reasoning, I have to work to filter through these reactions. A lot of the time, especially if I am triggered, I react before I can process. In that moment, I am unable to think clearly. Within that trigger, I might automatically go to fear or anger, even if that is not the appropriate feeling. It is hard to trust myself and my response in any moment. When this process is in action, it is difficult to get past the unconscious leap to fear and anger. Once I am in the fear and anger, rational thought is not how I respond to the interaction. Consequently, I do not respond at all to keep myself safe. I do not respond with fight or flight, I automatically freeze, as I did as a child.

In 1985, I was in a meeting with representatives from a company from which I was buying equipment. The engineer was rude and dismissive of me and my knowledge. He minimized my authority by referring to me as a bad cook who probably just opened cans to make meals. I was nonplussed. It was bizarre, as he did not know me; I thought, what does cooking have to do with machine tools? Apparently, as a woman, I upset his sense of the world order of men being in charge. He could not accept me as the one who knew what she wanted; I belonged in the kitchen. It took me completely by surprise and I had a hard time thinking clearly during the meeting. It triggered the helpless child for part of the meeting. I could not depend on myself to be coherent when under attack. I did not have any confidence that men would listen to my ideas and take them seriously.

I do not hate men. I fear them and I do not trust any man. Yet, my first response is to defer to men, even when I can see they are wrong, which can be infuriating. I begin to hate myself. My early programming is still strong. It is an ugly cycle where I trust too easily or do not trust at all. It is difficult to be in the moment.

There is a cyclical feeling to my contrasting understanding of trust. I go around the circle, trust too much, then trust not enough. I struggle to find the place that is rational. I feel this way about that person, so I trust this much. I try to base my trust on knowledge rather than letting it be an automatic response that was developed during the trauma of my childhood. It feels like a very closed system within me. It is hard to step off the circle of reaction and into understanding and determining who or what should be dependable.

I have to trust that people will drive the way they are supposed to, that they will follow the rules of the road, or I would be too frightened to go anywhere. I have to trust that manufacturers are using clean practices and materials that will not harm me. I would call this social trust. Understanding social trust is difficult, but much simpler than trusting on an individual level. Critical thinking can be applied. Research and knowledge can determine the level of trust. Professional trust is also easier to determine than personal. I can learn to trust co-workers by their actions. Do they do what they say they will? Do they finish their projects? This is a process that is dynamic and changing but easy to understand. It is challenging if I am triggered and unable to see past the pain of betrayal. Then my feelings are in charge and critical thinking is impaired.

Personal trust is entirely different. My past trauma, flashbacks, and triggers get in the way of trust. If someone has a certain smell, I might have a hard time seeing them clearly and will not want to be around them. Representations of the trauma are everywhere, and they undermine my thought process when they appear. Choice is betrayed and the past overshadows everything. My thought process is difficult to hear when my emotions from the past are engaged.

When Donald Trump was named president in 2017, I was completely triggered and sent back to the childhood place of danger and fear. I could not trust my government anymore. An accused rapist was now in charge, a man who denigrated and disregarded women and people of color in every way. In his speech and in his actions, he showed his utter contempt for women every day. My adult fear regarding the consequences of his being in charge was amplified by my childhood fear of not knowing what might happen next. I felt like my grandfather was back in charge of my life. How could I trust the world around me with a person who exemplified all of the negative traits of a privileged white man in charge?

Then add into that fear the number of people in our society who could support someone who actively derides and undermines women, even the many women who voted for him. It boggles my mind and triggers my fears to agonizing heights. I cannot trust anyone around me; they all feel like perpetrators. I am surrounded by the agonies of patriarchy. It must be horrific if you add the fears of a person of color within this construct. How anyone of any color or a woman could have voted for this belief system confounds my thought process. It does not compute.

This is the most difficult topic for me to articulate within the context of this book. As I sit here and think about it, my shoulders keep getting tighter and tighter. My heart shivers in protest. My stomach roils about. I want to curl up into a ball to protect myself. I want to hide. I have to work at pushing back my black space. It wants to take me into its protective aura. It does not feel like I have the words to explain what trust means to me or how hard it is to achieve.

My levels of trust have been attacked and derided by myself. I question whether I can trust anyone. How can I trust myself? I feel sick as I try to put words around it all. When I am with someone, how do I listen to my intuition and determine whether they are sincere? Can I tell if I am triggered and thinking through my emotions rather than with my rational mind? I usually can when I sit and think about what is going on inside. Yet, I have to take that time to determine who is in control, me or my past.

As a teacher, I have to trust everyone in my class to a certain degree. It is a necessity for me to be open to my students so that I can teach better. Within that, I am always questioning whether I am safe in the classroom, whether I can trust the students to listen and respond to what I am teaching them. I know that some students have been sexually abused, and that brings another level to my ability to trust. Can they hear me, or are they being triggered? I have to think about it all from their point of view and hope that I can share in a safe and empathic way so we can all be safe. If there are perpetrators in the class, how do I respond to that energy and keep the students and myself safe? There are many thoughts that have to be negotiated when out in the world, especially in a classroom.

Trust has many levels. It is a process of understanding that grows and evolves over time. Sometimes I learn that I cannot trust someone whom I thought I could. Other times, I find that I can trust someone more than I thought. When I give more trust to a person in error, it pushes me back to not being able to trust myself. There is, however, a sense of optimism that is present when I trust, a feeling that good things will happen, and we will accomplish what we set out to do.

I think everyone struggles with the concept of trust in the real world. I also feel that, as a survivor, my ability to recognize trust is impaired and I have to work harder to achieve it even when it is merited. Can I live without fear if I do not trust?

I do trust myself enough to take chances. I moved to San Diego without much of a plan, yet it worked. I decided to go to college for art, which was a big jump for me. I trust out of the belief that nothing can hurt me more than I already have been, or not very much. Sure, I could be raped, physically attacked, fail, or any number of other tragedies. My feeling is, so what? Been there, done that. I know I can survive it. I know I can heal. I trust myself to be able to persevere under whatever conditions present themselves to me. I would not want anything to happen, but I know that I would get through, as long as I was alive. I trust myself enough to drive across the country by myself. I have done that several times over the years to visit home in Michigan or my daughter or husband when they were on the East Coast and I was in San Diego. I am not afraid to be by myself. I have traveled to many places all over the world by myself. I like to be by myself.

As I have gained experience and healing has occurred over the years, I have come to a trusting place. I am better able to decide whom to trust and whom not to trust. I am able to listen to my inner voice when it says that person is unsafe, and then stay away. Sometimes, my voice says, yes, that person is whom she says she is and I can trust her. I can trust myself to know how to stay safe in most situations. It took a lot of work to get here. I still get it wrong or react in the ways I used to. There can be a lot of internal discussion to get to that healed space that allows more clarity.

The visual manifestation of trust is a harder one to develop. I think that the interaction with Nikki, in the body performance we worked on (discussed in Chapter 4), is one of the biggest steps I have ever made in the trust department. To be able to stay in my body and experience that interaction with her and expose myself in such a physical and open way takes a lot of trust on my part. To show her what those words feel like and to contemplate sharing those movements with the world is an extraordinary step for me. I am hopeful it will heal some of my self-esteem difficulties as it progresses. It is good for me to realize that I do belong in the world and have something to share that is important.

My armor series is about trust: how I trusted my psychological constructs to protect me. How the process of putting on this perceived armor was a place that was safe within the abuse. It was all internal and subconscious, yet I was safe within my body. Whatever was happening around me or to me, I would be able to survive. I was unaware of that construct when I created it. I was strong enough to build that psychological framework to protect my psyche.

I have sculpted a lot of the armor pieces; there are two different series. One is called *Armor: Memory Series* and the other is *Armor: Protection Series*. The *Protection Series* is constructed of leaves. Molds were made of leaves I gathered, which were then slip-cast to construct the body. The leaves were then molded around a female form, mine in some cases. For me, the woods felt like a safe place. The leaves represent that feeling I had when I was climbing a tree or walking through the woods, a beautiful place separate from the abuse. I still feel safest in the woods. Porcelain is the strongest of the ceramic materials, it is strong enough to protect my psyche. Similar to a psychological construct; it would not really protect me. It would break easily if someone hit it, but it has the presence and feel of strength, and is a metaphor for protection.

Image 8.1   *Armor: Memory Series #2*

The *Memory Series* is constructed of drawings I made with rolled clay. I used the bottoms of plastic containers to do the drawings in and made plaster molds from them. I then decided to color some with underglaze and leave some colorless. When using the slip, the underglaze releases from the mold and sometimes only brings part of the vibrancy with it. These are shadows of the underglaze on the image that I perceive as the vagueness of some memories. Some are very clear, others have only vestiges of hues on the image, and the rest have just the texture of the image itself. The form they are built into is again the female form, the torso, the center of the body, where armor is the most important.

This is a delicate process where time, knowledge, and experience are important. If I remove the mold form too soon, the structure of the sculpture will collapse. If I leave the mold form in for too long, the sculpture will crack apart as the porcelain shrinks and the mold does not. Sounds a bit like the healing process. Healing occurs in the right time and when you are strong enough to go back and look. Sometimes more knowledge is needed to get to that time when healing can happen. When I try to work on things that

I am not ready for in the healing process, it does not seem to work. I have to keep going back to that same thing and look at it over and over. If I push away from things that come up and do not deal with them when they are there, those things will stay there and interfere with everything else I am doing in my life. When I do not address things when the time is right and push them away, perhaps the eating disorder will pop up. Or I will begin to dissociate more, or feel like I can't cope with the world at all. Fear and anger can come to the surface in any given situation where it is not appropriate.

Healing is a delicate process also. I need to pay attention to myself and listen when my intuition or subconscious comes in and tells me I need to look at something from the past.

Image 8.2 *Armor: Protection Series #8*

CHAPTER 9

IDENTITY

Who am I? It would be nice to know how much of what I think was formed and programmed by my abuse. What would I be if the abuse never happened? Would I be more? Would I be less? These are questions I ask myself. Would I have made different choices, or would I have done all the stupid and good things in my life anyway?

I remember standing in line in kindergarten. The girl standing next to me, Louise, was a lot taller than I was. She looked comfortable, she talked to everyone else, and she did not look afraid. Was I different than her? It felt like I was different. I was afraid; I did not talk. I did not feel comfortable. She interacted with the other students in a free and happy way; she appeared playful and joyful. She smiled and laughed. At the time I did not know what joy was. I very rarely laughed. I smiled because everyone expected it. Smiling was one of my masks. My smiles were not genuine; I did not feel their joyous effects. At the time, I could not have defined what was different, but there was a feeling of difference. Louise was foreign to my understanding of the world. I could not see myself like her. I tried to be invisible.

Were our personalities simply different? Should all children feel joy and playfulness? I think they should. After the abuse began, I don't think I did. What is my personality? How different would it be now if I had not been abused? Would I be the same person? These are unanswerable questions. They keep me up at night sometimes; mostly I just try to move forward as I am.

Asking questions in this book is a milestone for me. For many years, I could not ask questions. I was not allowed. I could not question what was happening to me. It was not to be talked about. That took away my ability to ask questions about anything else. Without getting any answers, how did my identity develop? Did I have my own identity as a child? Was I just a sexual being, for someone else? Was I someone without wants or needs? Those needs would not have been met if I had had them anyway, so why have them?

In high school, there were flashes of me, I think. I was an activist during the Vietnam War, and I questioned the racial inequity around me. I was ten when Martin Luther King, Jr. walked, and I remember thinking how amazing he was to fight for rights in a peaceful way, as we watched it on TV. I was fiercely feminist in my reactions to the world as it was, as I still am now. I don't know if my reaction stems from my identity or from childhood abuse. Would my anger have manifested in those directions if I had not been abused? I was radical in pointing out unfairness and calling out bullies. I could fight for others, but not myself. I participated in my first sit-in when I was 14; it was 1969. I pushed against the restrictions placed on women and children by the religious speakers in the community. We should have had a voice and we did not.

Unfortunately, the alcohol and drug use pushed me into unsafe situations. I made a lot of poor choices—one of them was getting married at 18. It felt like the only way to escape, yet I could not escape myself. Instead of getting away from the trauma that formed me, I put myself into another abusive situation. There I was, feeling the same, just in a different location. Of course, my new husband pointed out how whatever I did "wrong" was all my fault. Too stupid, so he had to call me names; too slow, and he would have to hit me to get me moving. Again, in the same situation as when I was little: not in control and not able to be me. When someone is always berating you, calling you names, and being physically abusive, it is difficult to get a sense of who you are or who you could be .

I discovered that work was a safe place. I always had a job. I always excelled at whatever job I had. It was a good thing to be somewhere that I could be useful in a positive way. There were always male-domination moments. It was the 70s, after all. When I was a waitress, I would be approached as a sexual being. Customers were at times abusive, but I did not have to contend with that from management. Sometimes there were comments and sexual innuendos from fellow workers and from clients. I mostly just ignored them. No response is its own answer. In my first jobs, I worked in places with mostly women: for example, at a dress shop, and waitressing in a small family-owned business. When I went into drafting and design, some of the men dismissed me as a person. I was usually the only woman in the group.

My identity at the workplace was always as a smart, competent doer. I got things done. I solved problems. Other workers saw me as someone to confide in when things were not working. I kept their secrets, so they shared them with me. Then, I could try to find the solution to the problem. The men who worked in the engineering offices always knew what to do, so they never listened to the people who had to work with their tooling designs. I took the needs of the workers into account when I designed equipment or tooling. I always asked users what they thought was the best way to make something. They were the experts because they used the equipment every day. They made my job easier.

The worker aspect became a strong identity of mine as time moved forward, along with the sexually abused child and the abused spouse. Those latter two identities have interfered with and/or formed all of my other identities: the survivor, the activist, the student, the broken woman, the worker, the mother, the teacher, the feminist, and the artist. They sometimes all feel like they are different people. I put on whichever mask is needed at the moment. Whatever is underneath, whatever is me, is co-opted by the needs of others. I am very good at taking care of everyone else, not myself. I was not allowed wants and desires, so I did not develop them.

As I started making art, those wants and desires began to pop into being. It was scary, and I told myself, *No, no, no, you cannot want things; you will never get them anyway, stop it.* I fought against myself, pushing those feelings back down into the dark. *If I become aware, I will be in pain, push them away.* The creative process kept pushing me to the surface. It was demanding that I portray my voice. It was terrifying. The next twenty years were an exercise in healing, learning, and exposure.

I went back to school at the University of New Hampshire and subsequently went through a hospital experience and monumental healing discoveries in therapy. As I said earlier, I did research on alternate healing modalities, which I have continued throughout my life. I was always searching for what could help me. In this process, I discovered who I was, putting parts of myself together to form me. I imagine trying to write this back then; it would have been impossible.

Moving back to San Diego, when my husband was transferred again, was when my serious schooling in art began. It was a journey of discovery. Wow, I could create things. People actually paid attention to those creations. What a concept. I could say things visually that I never would have been able to verbalize at that time. I was creating myself at the same time that I was making art. I was making me. I went to community college part time for several years and finally committed to full time. Of course, I was not supposed to want or need anything, so I did it on the side. It moved into *I need to do this, and I need to do it for myself.* Healing had been happening until I was able to say, *I am going to get my degree and go to graduate school.* I was lucky enough to finish my degree at San Diego State University, and they accepted me into their graduate program. My husband and I had some difficulties at this time. I was changing. I was demanding to go a new way. Over time, we figured it out, but it was not pleasant at the time. He is now one of the strongest supporters of my work.

My thesis show was called *show and tell*. It is all work that demonstrated the sexually abused mindset. It is a metaphorical representation of the repetition—same shit, different day—of my childhood sexual abuse. *in the wind…* is the title of sixteen pinwheels in the wall, showing that childhood is dangerous, yet they felt joyful and free when I hung them. The pinwheels were constructed from porcelain, wire, nails, and wood. They were particularly dangerous-looking when you got closer. The wire and nails were sticking out of the center of the pinwheel and were sharp. The pinwheels turned, but the weight of the porcelain made them difficult to move. They were functional as a pinwheel, but not in any normal or reasonable way. They were too dangerous for children, yet beautiful, and children would want to play with them. The handles were embedded into the walls, so the wheels were scattered around the space as if the wind had blown them there.

Image 9.1 *into the wind…*

Childlike drawings were made with a plaster intaglio process using underglaze as ink and slip clay as paper. The molds were used to make the same drawing with different colors over and over. This represented the sexual abuse I experienced as a child. It was the same image, designating a different day; the abuse happened over and over, as did the images. All of the images were displayed on boards that had been painted black and worked as frames around the edges of the porcelain. Some of the images had been broken and pieced together on the boards. That indicated a day that was worse than the others. All the images were the same plaster molds; the colors used on each image were different and that designated the different days. The titles for these images are, *and in the beginning…*, *the world sees…*, *look it's…*, *into the…*, and *so the story goes…* I had a sense of completion when I put them up. It acknowledged the sheer volume of the abuse. Look how it happened in the past; it is no longer happening now.

Image 9.2 *and in the beginning…*

Image 9.3 *the world sees…*

Image 9.4 *look it's….*

Image 9.5 *into the…*

I constructed two books from those plaster intaglio pieces. The pages were put together with used baby pajamas that were cut out into children's toy images to hold the leaves of the books together. The covers were thin board covered with receiving blankets that I collected from thrift stores. The process of opening the books and turning the pages was uncomfortable as pages ground together and made grinding noises; the feeling was that they could break at any time. They were not easy books to read. The book titles were *once upon a time*…and *when there was….* There was a feeling of danger when you turned the pages, the way the components were put together amplified that impression of impending doom. This is delicate and I could break it if I am not careful.

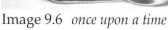

Image 9.6 *once upon a time*

Image 9.7 *when there was*

I constructed a large image out of handmade tiles, with large drawings in a childlike style on the interior tiles, and a frame of tiles that had small images on each tile, all drawings of stick figures. On the interior tiles, there were three very large images using sgraffito drawn into the tiles and using color with underglaze. They represented me at young ages, and were done in a children's style of drawing. It was called *oodles of sounds.* This work was ten feet tall and twelve feet wide. It overlooked the rest of the work in the show. The fragmentation of the images felt like me: parts put together to make a whole with the tiles not quite touching.

Image 9.8 *oodles of sound*

After the show, I took this work and set it on the retaining wall in my front yard. The children who walk past stop and look at the images and make up stories about them. They will tell their mom or dad those stories as they walk by. I have had several women stop and ask if my children or grandchildren made the images. I tell them no, I did, and here is what it is about. Two different women at different times started crying and told me their stories. They were also sexually abused as children. The connection was made. The art did its job and showed them they were not alone, and on some level, they recognized it before I explained.

Image 9.9 *Storyteller #5: listen to the silence*

In the *Storyteller* series, #5 is approximately three times life size and was a bust-like figure of a woman from under the nose to under the breasts. The front of the figure was a rough stoneware surface with no glaze. The back of the form is open so you could see inside the human form and into the arms. It was covered with white underglaze, and colorful children's drawings of monsters, people, and things on the surface. The inside represents the memories that the body has of past abuses. The figure sits on actual books I chose addressing aberrant sexual behavior or children's books. The entire piece is 57" tall x 76" wide x 67" deep. During the art opening thesis show, there were several children present. I provided crayons and paper for anyone who wanted to draw during the opening. The kids sat on the floor in front of the *Storyteller* and made up their own stories for her to tell. They would look at the book covers and the images on the inside of the back and respond to them. I was gratified by this interaction between viewer and art. There was an interplay and exchange between the piece and the children that was positive. They told their stories by looking at mine. It was called *listen to the silence*. It was a way of sharing, experiencing, and seeing with the children. For all the work in this thesis I chose the lowercase format on purpose. It felt like my interior child was the one who named them and that is the way she would write the titles.

Image 9.10   *Storyteller #5: listen to the silence,* detail

Image 9.11   *Storyteller #7: see the voice*

The Storyteller #7 was on a pedestal five and a half feet tall, high enough that adults had to look up at it. It was over my head, because I am short; it felt like a giant. I wanted to give the viewer the feeling of being a child while looking at it. This piece was life-sized from under the nose to under the breasts. The front surface was a bronze metallic glaze that felt shiny, dense, and opaque. The interior was coated with a white crawl glaze that was very rough and broken. The back had been pulled off of the figure and turned inside out. It had a representation of my face over and over. It was distorted from the construction process but visible. The faces were covered with the crawl glaze on the interior of the skin and the exterior skin had the bronze glaze. It was also placed on children's books and books that referenced deviant sexual behavior. The books were used as the framework for the idea of the figure as a storyteller. She is the keeper of the personal stories.

With the story boards in *and so the story goes…*, I have repeated the same images. This is an acknowledgement of the repetition of the abuse. Some of the images are broken and glued back together, like me. It is an image that shows the cycle of abuse, different day, still happening. Some of the images are in color and others are black and white representing that while the abuse occurs over and over, some days are worse than others.

Image 9.12   *and so the story goes…*

The final story is a self-portrait constructed from porcelain bowls and shards of bowls. Each of the pieces represent a year of my life and are screwed into the wall to form a pattern. Some of the bowls go out onto the floor; these represent my most current years and they are more intact. The other pieces are broken, different colors, or just porcelain colors; they are carved, torn, and formed. It is called *speak the story.* It is eight feet square and on a black background to show the white of the porcelain better. There is a sense of motion and change from beginning to end where the bowls come out into the space of the viewer.

I have described these works because the process of making them was also a process of making myself. Trying to represent the childhood sexual abuse visually allowed me a relatively safe place to think about the past. There were flashbacks. I cannot say how many critiques I cried through as I tried to verbalize what I was doing. It was a painful yet satisfying process. You can find the thesis *show and tell* at the SDSU Library.

This process of telling my story allowed me to see that, while I was sexually abused as a child, it is not who I am. It was a big part of what formed and molded me into who I am now, but I am not the abuse. Being able to see the work outside of myself is one of the more powerful healing moments in my life. I was able to differentiate *me* from what was done *to me.* I am forever grateful that I was able to get into graduate school and do the work.

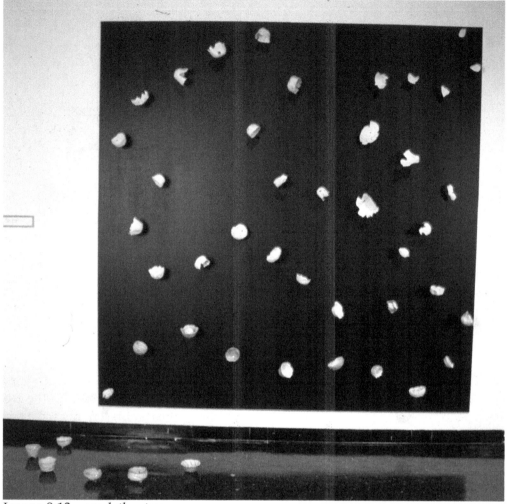

Image 9.13   *speak the story*

It seems that for me the process of discovering who I am is a lifetime endeavor. I discover new facets of myself as I move through the world as an artist and educator. My students have helped me see myself clearer in many ways. As they expose their stories, they help me define my own.

I taught in the local college and university systems as an adjunct for ten years after graduate school. State budget cuts took away those jobs, so I focused on my art after that. I began to volunteer at the Las Colinas Detention and Reentry Facility, a women's facility run by the Sheriff's Department. Eighty percent of the population there have said that they were sexually abused at some point in their lives. That is huge. I had other students there who told me they had been sexually assaulted and they had never told anyone else, so that eighty percent is not accurate. I encouraged them to talk about it and do artwork around the topic. I teach a class called *Expressing Trauma with Line*, which is a basic drawing class that culminates in a metaphorical self-portrait to represent their story as the last project. They do drawing projects that teach them how to draw and how to see. They build skills that allow them to tell their story in a clearer way.

To be able to watch others discover facets of themselves is amazing. When a student understands that yes, she could draw and draw well, I can see her self-confidence expand and grow into other parts of herself. It highlights my belief that art and the creative process are a healing endeavor. The process of looking at each other's art and talking about it amplified their understanding of the experience. I watched them see themselves in new ways, not just, "I am in jail, so I am bad."

Self-confidence grows as my students gain mastery and new skills. As they learn, they are able to look at new ways of making decisions and can see themselves as decision-makers. They see more clearly into themselves and are able to represent their feelings and ideas outside of themselves and process them in a different way.

My experience in the graduate program was a discovery of myself. The daily introspection to create visual imagery that represented my childhood sexual abuse experience allowed me the time and space to see myself. I had to push past many of the self-imposed blocks set up as a child for protection. Those blocks no longer serve as protection. They interfere with my knowledge of myself then and now. It is a struggle I have repeatedly to keep those blocks in the past.

I learn about myself through the process of creativity. I have also watched others experience this learning. It is a valid path of discovery for anyone. I was able to release myself from the specter of reaction and begin to choose who I wanted to be. For many years, I was just surviving and reacting to the world within the damage of the abuse. The reactions I made were not always in my best interest. They were just reactions. Fear was in charge and it pushed me into decisions that were not about me, but about the pain. I was unable to connect deeply with anyone, unable to feel the real or be in the moment. I was caught in the past. Art leads me into the future.

By using the ideas of the Healing Art Process, I did a project called *my feminist timeline*. It is basically my life in color. I was at a residency in France at the Center Pompadour: A Neo-feminist Laboratory. Artists, writers, filmmakers, musicians, photographers all come to have the time and the space to work on controversial topics as they wish.

My proposal was to do visual art around the history of feminism. I was unable to find very much information about this topic so I was having a hard time figuring out what to do. My second day there I woke up with the idea that my body is a repository for the stories that made me a feminist. So my life is feminist history in a nutshell.

I began doing a layout of my life looking at what happened to me in all the places I have lived. I made outlines and small sketches of that time line. Sexual abuse in Jackson, spousal abuse in Kalamazoo, and so on for all the places I have lived. The layout defined what the patriarchal society I live in had done to me.

I took that information and began doing color designs as I thought about what it had felt like to have all of these things happen. A beautiful abstract design began to emerge. I was using magic markers on a fiber material while at the residency. When I came home, I translated that into three oil paintings.[5]

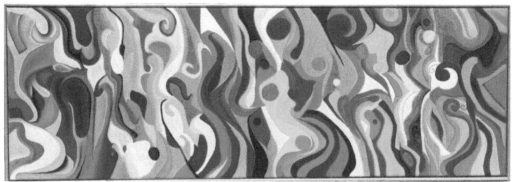

Image 9.14   *My Story in Color #1*

Image 9.15   *My Story in Color #2*

---

[5] There were two videos posted from interviews done while I was at Center Pompadour and you can see them here. Interview of Linda Litteral: m. spiegel at Centre Pompadour
https://www.youtube.com/watch?v=6MDignAR0oQ&t=10s
https://www.youtube.com/watch?v=4mXwDfIRe3s

Image 9.16   *My Story in Color #3*

CHAPTER 10

POST-TRAUMATIC STRESS DISORDER

In the preceding chapters, post-traumatic stress disorder (PTSD) has been a part of the conversation, though not named as such. The abuse is a flashback that pops up in my life at unexpected times. It is debilitating in many instances. The flashbacks were at their worst when I was hospitalized. I could not function in the world normally then. I found it difficult to be around people. I have had flashbacks my entire life. Mostly, I am able to keep them in an internal box, with minimal outward reaction, so others could not see them happening.

Are the voices in my head a part of PTSD? *I don't know.* Everyone has those negative voices. Some are less negative. They impact how I feel in any given moment. The voices are the different entities of myself that show up to chastise, criticize, and sometimes encourage me. Are these voices flashbacks or just the normal reaction to the world around me? Are they memories of other people's words that still impact me?

While writing this book, I have had moments when tears would start falling, and they would fall for several seconds. It is puzzling and strange. There is not a memory or feeling attached to the tears. They just fall. What am I crying about or why am I crying is mysterious. Is this a flashback? Do flashbacks consist of disparate parts that release at different times? Are they a feeling of intense sadness that is not attached to anything in the moment? Tears fall for no apparent reason. What has triggered them? Is the trigger from yesterday or a few minutes ago? Why is there intense anxiety for no apparent reason? It is all very confusing.

Sometimes I will be going along with my day and I stop and go somewhere else in my head. I do not have a picture of where I am. A few moments later, I realize I have not been in the moment, and so I continue with what I was doing before. I am aware of the disconnect after it has happened. When I was hospitalized, this disconnect lasted for hours—I would lose time and not know where I was. Now these times of disconnection are short in duration and less frequent. Yet it is perplexing, and I feel discombobulated in a mental and physical way when it happens, staring into space, frozen in time. Luckily, my subconscious is aware enough that these do not happen when I am driving or using electric tools. Maybe focus is a tool to avoid them.

I think the loss of moments are flashbacks of the abuse. I am reliving the event while still being disassociated from it. I exist in darkness and silence, as it happened in my childhood, in a blank and frozen place, separate yet there.

Intense anger sometimes pops up in my feelings for no apparent reason. Nothing has happened to make me angry, yet, I feel as if I would flame spray the world if I opened my mouth. I feel out of control and terrified of what I might do in these moments. I talk myself out of it in my head. Terror is another feeling that jumps out at me in strange moments. There is nothing that is threatening me that I can see. The terror is just there; my heart beats fast and my breathing elevates. It feels as if I am going to hyperventilate, knowing something horrific is going to happen at any moment. Nothing ever does. I feel the need to run but I can't, I'm frozen again. These feelings keep me from interacting with the world. I will stay home rather than carry that feeling with me into crowded situations. I do not always have the choice of sitting out of life, though. I have to go to work. I need to get to an appointment. It is a huge drain of energy to be normal when I don't feel that way. I get back home and collapse, unable to do anything for a time.

Again, I have to hide my reactions of the abuse to the world, still silenced.

The internalization of the abuse is complete. My body holds all of those feelings and they escape at strange times. Perhaps my injured child is telling me to be careful in the only way she can, by reminding me of the feelings I had at the time of the abuse, the emotions I did not or could not feel then. They were separate from myself during the moments of the abuse. It is the disassociation of all of those feelings connected to my body and escaping in the now.

It is difficult to verbalize these emotions and physical feelings that intrude on my everyday life. Words stumble and my innate sense of silence almost always wins. Who am I going to tell? In my experience, no one wants to hear about it. It is too foreign to their understanding of the world. I talk to my therapist about it. I have talked about it in group therapy also. It is difficult to describe, to allow myself to remember it and put words around it. I still have the overriding compulsion to stay silent. Do not speak; this is the way of abuse.

I think abuse continues because of the need to stay silent. The difficulty in speaking about something that is shameful and feels like my fault allows others to be abused. The only way to make change is to push past the silence and speak.

I think the utter randomness of the flashbacks is the worst. I cannot plan around them or predict when they may happen. They just do. Thankfully, they have been few and far between for a long time. Writing this book is stirring things up and pushing memories to the surface. Looking at it and thinking about it all is intense; the flashbacks seem to be waiting in the wings for when I relax, bringing tears, fear, and terror. My weekends seem to be a time of utter motionlessness. I cannot seem to get past the feeling of being still. I am not getting much done except the writing. It is what I have the energy for, not much else.

Gee, thanks Grandpa. While this is sarcastic, it is also the way I feel now. I would not be who I am and achieved what I have without the abuse. I like who I am now.

I sometimes wonder if there are boxes within my body. This box contains the first time my grandfather raped me. This other box is when he had his hand in my pants in the car. The next box is my reaction to the first box, sitting on the ceiling watching it happen. Another box is the reaction to the second box, the emotions I suppressed, and on and on, hundreds of internal boxes. Then, something happens that triggers me and another box is opened and I have to experience it once again: flashback.

I have been working hard to recognize what these trigger events are. It is difficult for me to see them clearly. I move so quickly to the flashback that I do not understand where the starting point is when it is over. If I could recognize triggers when they happen, I wonder—could I stop the flashback before it begins?

As I wrote in Chapter 4, I always have the visual images of the abuse, but the emotions and physical feelings were suppressed and disassociated from my body. When I have a flashback, it is sometimes a familiar image that has mental and physical feelings attached that I didn't know belonged with the picture. It is a connection that I didn't have in the past. The boxes find each other and it is with new understanding that I'm able to heal. In that sense, it is a relief to have them connected again. It is also terrifying and horrible to have to relive it over and over. I have not decided if I need to have these disparate parts connected again to heal. Am I able to feel emotions and physical pain within the picture? Can I then put it to rest? Or will the flashbacks keep jumping out and hijacking me even after the connections are made?

It is all very puzzling and scary. I relive events over and over. Sometimes it's just a picture; other times, it comes with a feeling attached, and another time has the physical sensations. Sometimes it comes with all three at once and it's like I'm there again. I move away from the now in every sense. How can I know what to do in this moment when I am forever stuck within a flashback? I can feel completely disconnected from myself and be stuck in the past. How do I escape the repetition of events? How do I stay present in the now? My brain deceives me by taking me to my past without my permission—I don't know what is causing the recession into the past.

I think all of the experiences explored in the previous chapters manifest into flashbacks at different times. In those chapters, I described them as the feelings that overwhelm me and put me into the past while I move through the world. The helplessness and fear, the shame and guilt, all of it can pop up and take over at any time. As my body remembers, it is not always by choice. When I smell a smell, I am transported to the past. When I descend into my black space, when I separate from myself or do not feel my feelings, it is not because I want to. It is because I have no choice and have been taken to the past by the past.

Writing this book, I am attempting to co-opt the PTSD and choosing to go back, to remember all of the ways that I experienced my survival of the abuse. I am remembering the psychological constructs my soul developed to save myself, beginning when I was three. I am exposing the struggle to stay in the conscious world, trying to recognize the triggers that take me back. I am taking the automatic jump to pain.

I am reminding myself that I survived the 2 a.m. terrors that dragged me from sleep, the embarrassment of being unable to speak, the tears that just sprout whenever, the inability to move or think, being lost in the past and unable to come back to the now, and the utter lack of control over my thoughts, feelings, and body.

A friend told me the other day that I was very brave for confronting my past, for exposing it all to the world the way I do. For me, it does not feel courageous; it feels like the next step. It is the necessary movement on my path to me. It just has to be done. I do not dwell on how hard it is; I protect myself as best I can and keep going. I have read many fantasy and magical books to distract myself from the reality of this book. I allow the mystical realms of someone else's imagination to protect me from my reactions to my hours in front of the computer, putting these words in the world.

I have minimized the trauma I experienced as a child my entire life; I am trying not to do that here. I want to recognize the depths of destruction that occurred to me from the abuse, and that after 60-some-odd years, realize I am still rediscovering parts of myself. My dissociation and denial all contribute to the PTSD I live with. In this process of honoring all of my past, I hope to mitigate the power of remembering. Perhaps the PTSD will abate and have less control over my day-to-day life.

I have always tried to numb my feelings, to stay separate somehow. It is easy to be dissociated from myself. I am always aware of who and what is around me. I am difficult to startle. Yet within that desire to forget has always been the window of remembering. I have flashbacks at unexpected and uncomfortable times. I remember the feelings and images when I do not want to. They jump up and surprise me, taking me back to the terror, the remembered physical annihilation of me. I have hidden this from everyone. I am trying not to hide any more. It did not work to be numb, so maybe exposure will. I need to honor all of the ways that I survived, all of the psychological pathways where my subconscious took me to keep me sane and able to function in the world. A lot of my methods were not choices. The numbness, the eating disorder, the drinking, the disassociation, the silence: they were necessary then. They are not now. I am attempting to retrain myself to allow the knowledge within me to be present, to know myself and no longer hide. It is a struggle, one worth making.

Friends have commented on how calm I am. I have developed that calm through trauma and terror. As I have needed to be silent about the abuse in the world, I have trained myself not to react and to only show the world my controlled face. Most situations do not scare me. My inner world does, and I am adept at hiding that from the outer world, even during a flashback. There is no screaming, no running; stillness hides.

There is a part of me that just knows. It is a realization of what is and what is not real. I am following this intuitive part of myself as best I can. For a long time, it was lost. By following that intuitive part, I feel more whole and at peace than I ever have. Honoring my inner knowledge, no matter what the world says, brings freedom and personal power. It does not matter what others think of me. I am within myself and beautiful.

The spiral journey I am on, where I look at the same thing again and again, yet move forward each time, is a powerful metaphor for healing. While earlier in the spiral, I had a lot more PTSD incidents, I know I am healing because they are less and less powerful as time goes by. There is a sense of calm within that has never been present before. It is a confidence in myself to travel that spiral and discover what is needed to move forward. To acknowledge the flashbacks and know that they are memories of terror and not the actual terror is to heal.

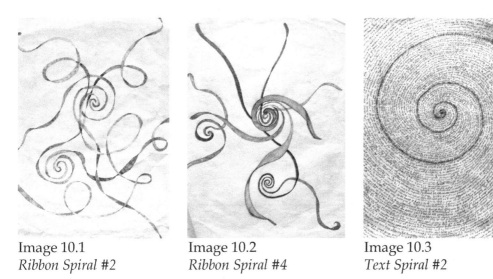

Image 10.1
Ribbon Spiral #2

Image 10.2
Ribbon Spiral #4

Image 10.3
Text Spiral #2

I have done many drawings of spirals representing me moving along my path— some are big, and some are small. Some of the lines are made with text, documenting my experience in words and images at the same time. Others have small drawings of memories and objects that make me think of the past navigating the spiral. Some are out in the world, earthworks that are ephemeral and will be erased as the wind, rain, and wildlife disperse them back into the ground. The drawings can look two-dimensional and flat, while others have perspective and look sculptural on the paper. There are spirals within the spirals, intertwining and moving apart to come back together again.

I was consumed by making spirals while at the Desert Dairy Artist Residency in 2020.[6] I was already there when the Covid lockdown began. I decided to stay for the entire three-week residency, as it was pretty safe there with very few people around. I drew spirals with pencil, markers, ink, ash, sand, rocks, etc. Whatever I thought about or did had spirals in it during that time. It was a journey of looking at my life and how I have traveled through it. My healing journey was one of moving forward and up, and then moving backward and down, to heal the same thing in a different way or from a different view.

When I went for walks, I would draw spirals in the sand or make them with rocks and sticks found in the environment. It was a physical journey as much as a psychological and emotional one. I found myself thinking a lot about my life and where it has been and why I was where I was in the moment, and how I had arrived there. The way to express it all visually was to make all of the spirals that I did.

Image 10.4 *Spiral Movement #3*   Image 10.5 *Spiral Movement # 8*

The Mojave Desert is a beautiful place, with open sky, strange and wonderful critters, and beautiful flowers at the right time of the year. It is conducive to peace and

---

[6] Interview with Linda Litteral: Ted Meyers at Desert Dairy Artist Residency
https://www.youtube.com/watch?v=TyJW69LcgyI

contemplation. The opportunity to go there and work on my art was wonderful and an important avenue for growth and healing for me.

During this time, I was also making small porcelain carvings with spirals that I would place out in the environment before they were fired. They would then eventually collapse back into clay particles and be spread by the wind and rain. There are still remnants of those to be found now. I did fire some of the carvings in a fire pit where we would cook dinner on some evenings. I saved the ash and then used that ash to make a large spiral in the sand.

The spirals also represent the way that PTSD has worked in my life, moving me around the circles of my experience, and pushing me back to the past with flashbacks while trying to live in the now.

Image 10.6 *Spiral Movement #18*

CHAPTER 11
DON'T SHUT UP

I think that there are many different situations in our patriarchal world that cause a lot of the symptoms I have been discussing. Our world has very little compassion or care for anyone other than privileged white males: for example, for women, people of color, LGBTQIA+, the homeless, refugees, girls sold in marriage, trafficked people, slaves, and on and on. The way we talk about each other, the words we choose to describe ourselves and others, these are important. Words have an inherent authority when they come from the patriarchy. Whoever thought up the ditty "sticks and stones will break my bones but words will never hurt me" had it so wrong. I think words are very damaging when used against us.

Once we hear a negative voice telling us what is wrong with us, it is in our heads forever. Add physical, sexual, and/or emotional abuse and the words are amplified.

Words are used to define and label who and what we are. We are in charge (patriarchy) or we are other. This can be damaging to our psyches. If you hear that you are a piece of ass enough times, it sinks in. It is hurtful and hard to push out of our thoughts. It makes us lesser. Words put us in boxes; they constrain our ability to move in the world. Once you are labeled, it is difficult to change that label. *You are mentally ill. You are fat. You are useless. You can only be a sexual being. You are stupid, etc.;* the naming goes on and on.

Advertising is a perfect example. Here are magazines, television, and movies all telling you that you need to buy this to be something better. Use this product and you will be more. All of this is telling you that there is something wrong with you. Those represented are the ideal, making all the rest of us the other. After hearing and seeing this over and over, it is difficult to deny it to our subconscious. It is harmful to the individual and to society. This is capitalism at work. This trauma affects everyone.

Then, think about the bully who calls you stupid, fat, or ugly over and over. These are individual attacks that seep into our pores and our psyches. There is the parent who does not encourage, but only derides; the teacher who does not see you as important enough to teach; the guy who hoots at you on the street and uses sexual words to describe you; the grandfather who tells you to be quiet. I have experienced all of these things. They all have had an influence on how I think about myself.

Secrets are dangerous. How do we fight back?

How many children commit suicide because of sexual abuse?

How many adults commit suicide because of sexual abuse?

How many women drop out of high school or college because of rape? I personally know five women who did and talked to me about it.

How many people go to prison because of the damage done to them from childhood sexual abuse? Isn't it obvious that if 80% of a jail's population has been sexually abused, it must have had an effect on their behavior that caused them to be incarcerated? Maybe if there was no child abuse, we would not need prisons.

How many people need therapy because of childhood sexual abuse?

How many people have physical ailments caused by childhood sexual abuse?

I would bet we have no idea. Most children do not tell anyone about the sexual abuse. Many women do not report rape. Many men do not expose themselves as victims of sexual abuse. I would include every gender here. Sexual abuse victims have no gender bias; the abuse is all-inclusive.

As a society, we spend millions of dollars on the results of sexual abuse. In our capitalistic society, the loss of income would be monumental if we solved the problem of sexual abuse. So, why would that society want to heal sexual abuse? It makes money. It should be important enough to talk about. It should be important enough to change. That is a minor concern compared to the damage that is done to the children and the results of that harm. The root of a problem usually grows over time if it is not addressed. We should address sexual abuse as a societal problem that needs to be changed, both in the way we think about it and the words we choose to use to talk about it. What is the difference between she was raped and he raped her? Each statement implies fault. Was the fault hers or his? What is the difference between the definition of incest (two people who are related and having sex) and sexual abuse (someone stronger forcing sex on someone weaker)? She caused the rape, or he did the rape? How do you think we should talk about rape as a society? *The child was seductive.* No child is knowingly seductive. In court cases, why is this a word used over and over to describe a child? It implies fault. *She asked for it.* This is wrong and disgusting. That any adult can even say this implies a dangerous mindset that is part of the problem. The world is androcentric: look it up. It is a word that defines our society and most of the world.

The damage to our society is just as widespread as it is to the victim. Abused children use every ounce of their energy just to survive. They miss many of the important lessons that children need to learn to live and share within society as a positive member. Instead, they are self-medicating, running away from home, or living in dangerous situations, such as being involved in prostitution and joining gangs to get by, with a large number of them ending up in prisons and jails. It is a total drain emotionally, fiscally, and spiritually on our society that could be minimized if society would recognize the importance of taking care of our children.

As I stated earlier, one of my ways of not shutting up is to teach art at the local women's detention center, Las Colinas, run by the San Diego County Sheriff's Department. I developed a class called *Expressing Trauma with Line*, a beginning drawing class formatted to allow students to learn how to show the world their feelings in a safe and supportive way. Eighty percent of the population there has admitted to being sexually abused at some time in their life. Using drawing, I see them grow in self-esteem and self-awareness. They can communicate a part of their life that they never had before. The final project is a metaphorical self-portrait that is always empowering for them to complete. I have also taught art at R.J. Donovan Correctional Facility, a California state men's detention center under the auspices of a group called *Project Paint*. Many of the students have also revealed sexual abuse in their pasts.

One of my students had lost her job and her ability to ever work again in her field because of drugs. She was in the facility. We were doing a drawing class on negative space. She was struck by the total annihilation of herself within the idea of negative space. By using and stealing drugs, she felt she had negated whom she wanted to be, and ended up being incarcerated. We talked through the idea that by showing the negative space, we were defining the positive space. It was illuminating. The loss of innocence and the feeling of being out of control in life because of sexual trauma needs to be shouted to the rooftops.

Patriarchy is complicit in the societal acceptance of sexual assault. When Donald Trump was elected to the presidency, I was appalled: a man accused of sexual assault numerous times. I heard an interview with him years before with Howard Stern. They were talking about Trump's thoughts about his daughter. His perception of her was abusive and wrong. He was perfectly okay with Stern calling her a "piece of ass"; he said he would date her himself if she were not his daughter. How is this okay? There are many quotes from Trump about women and how he loves to abuse them. "Grab 'em by the pussy," "beautiful piece of ass," or "you have to treat them like shit." He denigrates women and reduces them to being only a body.

I had not been in therapy for many years, but at that time, I felt unsafe and went back. Trump reminded me so much of my grandfather, and now he was in control of my country. I was triggered back into a place of no control and no safety. Many people support him; consequently, they are all perfectly happy to ignore sexual abuse. I find this an indictment against patriarchy. Go to Wikipedia and search "Donald Trump sexual misconduct allegations" to see information about the 26 women who have filed against him.

The gross and factual truth about white male privilege and our society that ignores it is that if you are white, it is okay to abuse women and children sexually. If you are rich, it is okay to abuse women and children sexually. If you are in a position of power, you can sexually abuse women and children. If you are a man, you can sexually abuse women and children without any repercussions.[7] Heaven forbid we ruin a young man's life by holding him accountable for his actions, or a father who was seduced into fucking his three-year-old. I remember reading about a case in Texas some years ago where the judge gave a father custody of his young daughter after saying she seduced him into sex when the mother took him to court for sexual abuse. White male privilege and patriarchy are the instigators of these ideas. These moments are a travesty of justice. That our society accepts these kinds of actions is proven in the highest offices in our country. Both Clarence Thomas and Brett Kavanaugh of the Supreme Court were accused of rape and/or sexual misconduct during confirmation hearings. I found the victims to be much more credible than the men, yet they were confirmed as justices. This is a gross abuse of the justice and political systems. They will be able to adjudicate cases against women and for men for the rest of their lives: the patriarchy at work.

The feelings I experience from the examples above take me straight back to the sexually abused little girl who has no place in the world except as a sexual being to be used by men. We have to speak up. We need to change how girls and women are perceived globally. We need more women in places of power. There is so much creativity and life just thrown away by the abusers in our society. Innocence is lost. Safety is only a construct for men. As women or girls, we expect to be attacked and seen at fault when in those situations. It is difficult to feel safe in a world that thinks this way. I never feel safe.

The church is another patriarchal construct that keeps women and children in their place. There is documentation that the Roman Catholic Church knew priests were sexually abusing children. They kept moving the priests around to hide what was happening. There have been accusations of abuse occurring in many congregations. The Mormon's Church of Jesus Christ of Latter-day Saints is another institution with many abuse allegations. The majority of church doctrine has been developed to keep women and children in places of control by men. Women are not allowed any power within the religions of Orthodox Judaism, Islam, or most sects of Christianity, to name the largest ones. Unless there is an equal division of power within these religious constructs, it is harmful and dangerous to us all. We need to expose the abuse that is happening.

I remember when I first read *The Color Purple* by Alice Walker. What an amazing story of abuse and recovery. It was difficult for me to see the words on the pages at times. I had to keep going back and rereading to hear what she was saying. Yet, it was a public affirmation of a child's journey through abuse. The work acknowledges the damage and the strength of the child to persevere and be in the world and live.

---

[7] I realize these are generalizations and there are exceptions, but those are far too few.

I was happy that an author had the strength and commitment to put this taboo subject into the world. Also, in *Forrest Gump*, there is another story about the sexual abuse of a young girl and her difficulty in growing up without harming herself. When I read or hear about the movie, I find that the abuse is the least talked-about part of the story. The taboo around talking about sexual abuse is stronger than the one about it happening. If we don't talk about sexual abuse, we can ignore it as a society. If it is not verbally in the public sphere, then it's okay. If I don't have to hear about abuse, it is not happening. Yet, it happens all the time. As a society, we need the images and the words in front of us to be able to change.

There are multiple platforms that have statistics about the rape of both girls and boys. They all say that the numbers are incorrect, as a lot of abuse is not reported. A victim sometimes never tells.[8]

As ordinary citizens, we can bring the topic up in our schools or in any situation where questions are pondered. We can bring it into the open so the world can express what it is and talk about how it can be stopped. Laws should be implemented to protect victims. The acceptance of "boys will be boys" should be eradicated. How do we raise our children? How do we change the current paradigm that allows it all? We fight against the patriarchy and the tenets that define it.

By writing this book, I am raging against the norm, against the taboo of exposing ourselves and our rapes to the world. We are supposed to be silent and take it. While this taboo has been opening up slowly to scrutiny my entire life, it is still in control. If the leader of our country can have 26 people accusing him of rape or sexual misconduct and still be the leader, that tells me no one cares whether he raped any woman. It does not matter. Those women do not matter. It is a negation of our voices. We must keep pushing against this norm and change it. Society will never progress until we do. We will stay in the same male-centric place of violence where no woman is safe.

Brett Kavanaugh, Clarence Thomas, Olivier Duhamel, Bill Cosby, Jeffrey Epstein, Donald Trump, Kobe Bryant, Michael Jackson, Harvey Weinstein, James Toback, Brett Ratner, Les Moonves, and on and on—the list is endless. They were all accused of sexual assault or sexual misconduct, and these are just names we recognize. As public figures, these are the ones who give the rest of the men permission to behave however they want toward women and children. It should be illegal to pay off a victim so they retract their case against the perpetrator. It is against the law to sexually assault a child (or anyone), period. It is against the law to rape, period. Yet, the culture of rape is alive and well in our society, and unless we keep fighting back, it will never change. *Do Not Shut Up.* The

---

[8] Platforms with information related to this are https://www.rainn.org/, https://www.cdc.gov/injury/features/sexual-violence/index.html, or https://ucr.fbi.gov/crime-in-the-u.s/2018/crime-in-the-u.s.-2018/topic-pages/rape

platforms #BalanceTonPorc (French; Squeal on your Pig) or the American #metoo are necessary. Keep squealing. Maybe something will change and your children will be safe.

For me, the exposure of my abuse through art is a powerful thing. It gives my victimization gravity and importance. It turns my victimization from a thing of shame and misery into a statement of survival and renewal. The significance of what the abuse altered in me is revealed and transformed into strength. The utter destruction in my deepest self is rebuilt to recover some of what was lost. The communication and sharing of the results of my abuse is a tempering of the strength I have gained through the work I have done to heal. I cannot shut up. I will not shut up.

I used the words of the poems that are placed at the beginning and the end of this book to construct these three self-portraits. They are images of me at the ages of two, seven, and seventeen. By inscribing the poems on my body, and defining my body with the poems, I attempt to take control of the results of my sexual abuse. Looking at myself as these words allows me to look at the changes I've made through healing, and move back in time to look more clearly at how the abuse changed and formed me. All of the results of abuse that I speak about in the book are a part of who and what I am today. This is a metaphorical tattoo of what I experienced, another way of not allowing the world to silence me.

Image 11.1
Don't Shut Up #1

Image 11.2
Don't Shut Up #2

Image 11.3
Don't Shut Up #3

I did a show in Linköping, Sweden about art, healing, and incarceration. Kathleen Mitchell and I presented art from our students from Robert J. Donovan Correctional Facility. We then did art around our reactions to working in that facility. We did personal work and a collaboration piece. Sharing their work gave them a voice in a new way. They are working to change their world through art.

The women at Las Colinas Detention Center shared a paragraph with me about what the art class meant to them. I was not allowed to take any of the art they did out of the facility. I did a catalog of their words to share at the show. Using their words for the lines, I drew a female figure for the cover of the catalog. This allowed them to have a voice in a new way, and served as another way to give them confidence and importance in the world at large.

Image 11.4   *Words from Las Colinas*

Art allows transformation and it improves the confidence and sense of self-worth of the prisoners. It gives them a voice and we were able to share that with a larger audience. Another way to express *Don't Shut Up* no matter what your lived reality is.

CHAPTER 12

ART AS SOCIAL DISCOURSE
AND AN AVENUE OF CHANGE

A rt is a vehicle that raises awareness in the viewer's consciousness. Art is communication at a more fundamental level that is portrayed through visual imagery. The impact of the visual image touches on the emotions at the same time that the intellect is engaged. This dual jolt has a better chance of sneaking past our preconceived notions about the world and allows for a change in our belief systems.

> The artist desperately seeks to engage the mind and spirit of the spectator, to bring him to a state of awareness that will permit no evasion…knowing that art is more than embellishment and that it can make visual man's follies and estrangement.[9]

Through personal experience or my story, I bring viewers' attention to a visual voice about childhood sexual abuse. With art as the vehicle, viewers can question their notions of what this social problem means to them. Once an idea is brought to our attention, it is challenging to ignore questions the issue may raise that occur within ourselves. Awareness and education are the catalysts that bring about new views of an issue, and change will result.

> Social conscience is a major and recurring theme in the history of Western art. Throughout the ages there have been artists who, as perceptive observers of the affairs of humanity, have refused to remain indifferent to the social and political conditions affecting their fellow humans. Over the centuries, their work has

---

[9] Schwartz, 2000, p. 7

stood as an impressive monument to the social and ethical conscience of humanity.

These artists have shared an awareness of the often harsh and unpleasant realities that make up the human condition. A serious consideration of their work reminds us of these realities, but at the same time, their work points to the possibility of social transformation and transcendence of those oppressive features of human existence.[10]

With the visual voice, the silence inherent in the manifestation of sexual abuse is broken. By breaking this cycle of silence, a dialogue begins between the viewer and the art that affects the thoughts and beliefs of those who see, hear, or speak the story. The child's drawings that are depicted in my body of work have been influenced by case studies of children who have been sexually abused and are involved in art therapy programs. This draws attention to the fact that this story is not only mine. Sexual abuse is repeated on many children in our society. Sexual abuse occurs to the same child again and again. That is how my story goes. The visual repetition of an image and its story in my work echoes the repeated offense. My choice of lowercase letters in some titles is to emphasize how common sexual abuse is among children. The more people see that this is true, the more chance for change and protecting our children.

Successful works of art enhance, destroy, or transform common assumptions, perceptions, and categories, yielding new perspectives and changed insights, although they sometimes reinforce conventional assumptions as well. They can transfigure experience and conceptions, calling attention to aspects and meanings previously slighted or overlooked…

Works of art are critical in generating powerful conceptions because they provide insights that are closely linked to emotional responses and are therefore likely to reappear in similar situations. Part of the meaning of artistic talent is the ability to sense feelings, ideas, and beliefs that are widespread in society in some latent form, perhaps as deep structures or perhaps as unconscious feelings, and objectify them in a compelling way.[11]

The art is observed, and viewers are compelled to look at their way of seeing the world and question its validity. The feelings and thoughts accessed through this process let viewers contemplate their own beliefs. By integrating intellect and emotions, art can be a powerful tool for social or political change through personal belief systems.

---

[10] Von Blum, 1976, p. 1
[11] Edelman, 1995, p. 52

As a survivor of sexual abuse, moving the thoughts, memories, and emotions from inside me and projecting them into a piece of art so that I can look at them removed from my body is transformative. I can see them more clearly without the feelings my body experiences when I think about the sexual abuse. It removes me from the debilitating reactions that the abuse engenders. The work itself can trigger more memories, yet it is not as dangerous as when the thoughts, memories, and emotions are only encased within my body. It propels me to create more work to expose the secret.

Translating damage into art and exposing it to the world is powerful. Breaking the silence visually is another way to heal yourself whole. That is how it works for me. Words have always been dangerous. Keeping the secret for so many years and being silent affected my ability to function through words. When I discovered artmaking, it was *WOW! I can say things without words. What an amazing concept.* It was still difficult to break my silence, yet the artmaking process opened up speaking in a new and compelling way. I could see the emotions right there in front of me. They could not hurt me there, or not as directly anyway.

The viewing of art about incest is just as powerful. I healed by looking at others' thoughts, memories, and emotions, which they communicated through art about their abuse. By exposing cultural, personal, and social ills, communities can be healed through the art that is made about them. The process of exposure, of showing what is hidden, and the communication of the story to others is healing in and of itself for the artist and the viewer. Both personal and cultural damage that is shown through art is healing.

Little as we know about the way we are affected by form: by color and light, we do know this, they have an actual physical effect. Variety of form and brilliancy of color in the objects presented to patients are actual means of recovery. People say the effect is only on the mind. It is no such thing. The effect is on the body too.[12]

Through making art and reading about healing through art, I began to see how it was helping me live my story instead of hiding behind it. Creating art that exposes my painful history transforms my experience into a monument of healing. Throughout my artistic life, I have been able to begin to understand some of my pain and how to turn it into beauty by sharing it visually. My journey through art has been intensely personal. That process of looking inward has healed many parts of my injured self. Within that internal process, I have discovered the universal experiences that connect me to others.

Humans are creative beings. That a rational person can dismiss the arts as unimportant is deluded. We should nurture and celebrate the creativity of our children. When we honor our creativity, we are more connected to each other as a community.

---

12 Nightingale, 1859

When we use color and image to express our emotions, we are able to transform the energy of those emotions to a higher level of consciousness. If we rage and share that rage with images, music, dance, and poetry, we can sublimate the need to destroy and experience the chance for change. Fear is real in our world and can cause destruction. When we take the energy of fear and make imagery that shows its reality, it exposes the possibility of a different way of living. We can use the energy of fear and transform it into healing and beauty through creativity, which will push us toward life and community. By taking our gut feelings and expressing them in a vision of what is felt, it can point out what can be changed.

As I create art and connect to my internal self, I am reaching out to the world to share my experience. Through metaphor and symbolism, I am exposing the results of sexual abuse for all to see. This process connects me to all sexual-abuse survivors, as we have all experienced the emotional upheaval that sexual abuse engenders. By defining my story visually, I can unveil new ways of experiencing it in the world. When I make those feelings visual outside of my body, I can see the path to change within myself.

> I thought of art as the expressive creativity of a soul struggling to self-actualize...The works of art I write about here have all had a transformative impact on my life...examples of the ways in which beautiful works of art have concretely and constructively influenced my thoughts, my habits of being...As we critically imagine new ways to think and write about visual art, as we make spaces for dialogue across boundaries, we engage a process of cultural transformation that will ultimately create a revolution in vision.[13]

Art is the opportunity for anyone to be free, to be able to use their creativity to communicate clearly what is supposed to be silent. Art can transform our personal feelings and change our external outlook of the world, both when we are making art and when we are experiencing someone else's vision of what it feels like to be in the world. Art can confront thoughts and emotions in a safe way. It allows the viewer to look at concepts that are troubling or taboo. It gives us the space to question our worldviews and change them from within, an internal and intuitive transformation. By experiencing art, we inform our souls, whether by doing or seeing.

Art is the expression of the artist's perspective, yet it has the possibility to change the world's view. It can show the possible range of emotions for any human being. By exposing human emotion, viewers who are cut off from their inner selves can recognize those feelings and begin to know. Those who are connected and balanced can revel in those feelings. It can be a process of self-discovery and peace. Our inner eye can see what

---

[13] hooks, 1995, pp. xi-xvi

has been lost and recover it. The perspective revealed during the creative process can be subconscious; the artist's hands expose the truth of themselves in the process of making. The creative drive is a human need.

> Artists have known intuitively what others are just beginning to discover: creating a visual image on paper or canvas, with clay or through any art medium, can produce physical and emotional benefits for both the creator and the viewer. And now thanks to extensive research in the fields of split-brain functioning, visualization and psychoneuroimmunology (study of the emotions and the immune system), we are finally able to understand how this powerful healing tool can be used by anyone, even those without the slightest trace of artistic ability, to create profound changes in their lives and activate healing at the deepest levels.[14]

We are creative beings. We do not have to have the title of artist to create and heal ourselves and heal others. The process of creating, of using color, sound, word, or body movement to express what we feel, is healing on many levels. There is joy in the creation, community in the process of sharing, and understanding as we contemplate that which we have made. I think that those categorized as "without the slightest trace of artistic ability" have been programmed and blocked from their natural human creative process. Trauma and patriarchy cut us off from that joyous expression at an early age as we are damaged, and our ability to reach our inner eye is impaired. Society teaches us that art is not important, but art and creativity are imperative to our mental and physical well-being. Everyone should have a creative outlet to know themselves better. I think it is the pathway to healing the world's level of hate and poverty. Heal individuals, allow them expression, and the world changes. Through the creative process, there is hope and optimism.

The languages of creative process are universal. We are born with them. We intuitively know how to use our bodies to move in joy as children. When we are allowed to express ourselves with our crayons, we are following our deepest knowledge of our inner view. When we build our mud pies, we are sharing our uniqueness and commonality with each other and ourselves. As we run and scream and swing our arms in play, we are whole within the joy of movement and sound.

As an artist, I search for and strive to find that feeling of wholeness and express it to the world, to lay open the damage and find the way to healing, to show viewers they can move past the trauma and damage to feel. Art is a subversive action that protests against the status quo. It is a defiant act to reveal the truth. Within the process of exposure, healing begins. The silence can be put on display.

---

[14] Lyshak-Stelzer, 1999, p. 1

I was taught as a child to hide what I actually felt and show the world a mask. What I was feeling was unacceptable to the adults around me, so I buried the emotions deep. I built block after block to keep my reactions from showing. This process of creativity is my digging into that depth, exposing what has been hidden from myself. The definition of art for me is revealing to the world what needs to be seen compellingly.

Art and the creative process is a prescription for health and healing. The damage to the psyche from childhood sexual abuse is obscene. It lasts forever. It affects how we see ourselves and how we act in the world. One of the most powerful acts of revolt against the damage for me is the creation of what is in my mind's eye, to communicate what my psyche has endured and share that with others. It gives me back myself. Within that personal motivation is the added prize of social change, to be able to attain understanding through viewing and disrupt the trope of silence around incest. My art can show that the victim is to be protected, not the patriarchal construct of debasement for control. Within that paradigm shift, society can also heal.

Image 12.1   *The Walk*

As I mentioned in Chapter 10, I arrived at Desert Dairy Artist Residency on March 13th, 2020. The residency is located in 29 Palms, near the Joshua Tree National Monument. The first stay-at-home order as a result of the Covid-19 pandemic began on March 19th, 2020. I chose to stay in the desert until my residency time was completed. The artwork I focused on were spirals, in drawings, in clay sculpture, and constructed in the environment with natural materials, stones, drawing in sand, and ash from wood fires. The largest spiral was a labyrinth made of ash that you could walk into your center and then return. It was a meditation in movement through the spiral space.

Spirals have been in my work for a long time; they show up in paintings and sculptures. The possibility bowls that I carve have them often. The spiral for me represents my healing process throughout my life. I am an incest survivor and rape survivor. The process of healing has been a long road and that road spirals forward and then spirals back as I must look at things again. In my art, it is representative of strength, power, and beauty.

I was walking around the yard one day with Anna Stump, the owner of Desert Dairy, and I said it would be cool to have a spiral labyrinth on the property. She thought about it for a little bit and said, "Let's do it." I began to think about the design and what I would want to make it like.

When I arrived home after the residency was completed, I researched spirals in history and came up with the triskeles form which is a three-legged spiral. This was used on ancient Greek shields as a form of protection. My intention for the labyrinth spiral was for it to be a place to inspire creativity, bring abundance, and provide a safe space for women. All you have to do is take the first step and walk into the space. Anna devoted a square of 80 feet in each direction to the project in the backyard of Desert Dairy.

I invited the Feminist Image Group (FIG), a group of feminists who are professional artists who support each other in San Diego, to be a part of the project. Several artists chose to submit work to the project and all those and others donated to cover constructions costs. Nilly Gill, Judith Parenio, Amanda Saint Claire, Cindy Zimmerman, Kathy Nida, Minnie Valero, Anne Olson, Moya Devine, Kirsten Aaboe, Stacie Birky Greene, Helen Redman, Janice Grinsell, Anna Stump, Susan Osborn, Kathy Mitchell and myself all donated work and/or funds to the project.[15]

Most of the work is clay, since I gave artists clay to work with and many of them had used the medium before, so they were good to go. Others I coached through the process and then I fired and glazed all the work that was not fired by the artists. There is artwork placed throughout the legs of the triskeles that you can contemplate as you walk the labyrinth. Other work is made from paper-mâché, glass, and poetry.

---

[15] If you visit the Feminist Image Group Facebook page you can see images of all of the art donated and artist statements.

As I was building the work I was going to put into the labyrinth, I constructed a small spiral labyrinth in my garden. It has a smaller three-foot Maquette of the larger totem that I built first to decide on construction of the larger piece.[16]

I built an eight-foot-tall totem that rests in the center of the three legs. There are possibility bowls at each corner of the legs and in the spirals at the entrance of the space. In the first leg as you enter the space there are tiles that represent the colors and stones of the chakras. You move from the earth chakra and on to the root, sacral, solar plexus, heart, higher heart, throat, third eye, crown, and higher crown chakras as you walk the leg. This represents moving from your physical body into your meditative space as you walk the spiral. When you leave the labyrinth, you walk back down the chakras on the other side of the leg and symbolically move back into your physical body. There are smaller spiral totems at each corner of the knees that I constructed.

As you walk the legs you see the artwork that is embedded in the rocks of the form. Most of the art has been epoxied onto concrete pedestals so it is lifted above the rocks and easier to see. My husband Lance Reynolds did the concrete pedestals for me. The poem "Mulch" by Nilly Gill was written in English and Hebrew. The English version is under the rocks of the first leg written on rice paper in a long line to follow the form. The Hebrew version is under the third leg also on rice paper written in a single line.

Image 12.2   *The Walk,* detail

---

[16] You can see it on my Instagram page at @lindalitteralartist.

Judith Parenio built a tall rabbit *Milk for All* that has multiple nipples to feed the world. Amanda Saint Claire did several small figures that have small pools attached to collect water for the local fauna when it rains. Minnie Valero did three goddesses, *Venus of Willendorf, Isis,* and *Pachamama.* Susan Osborne did a tile with the goddess of the labyrinth, *Ariadne.* Kathleen Mitchell did two glass pieces called *Spirals* and *Three Sisters* representing growth and rebirth. Ann Olsen did tiles that represent female power, birds, sun, planets, balance, and indicators of progress and discovery. Kathy Nida did a figure of a slightly exploding female form. Janice Grinsell did *Life's Breath,* to represent life's chances we take. Moya Devine completed a series of masks called *Alvar of Alviso* that were begun by her student Alvar who was killed in a car accident. Cindy Zimmerman did *Rose Rocks,* representations of mineral formations found in her home state of Oklahoma. Kirsten Aaboe did a four-sided pyramid with symbols, of which some are for joy, protection, strength, and journey. Stacie Birky-Greene did *The Three Fates* to represent the cycles of life and *Endangered Arroyo Toad,* which guards the east leg of the labyrinth. Nelly Gill wrote the poem "Mulch."

I went out to the Dairy in October, 2020 to measure and lay out the form in the space. I put posts and lines to define the triskeles with the dimensions I had figured out beforehand. I began gathering rocks from the surrounding area. It is an area where dirt bikes go all the time and is pretty messed up. It was still hot so I was going into the desert at 6:00 in the morning and collecting until around 9:00 when it became too hot. I began the form by defining the entrance and all the corners at this time. In November I spent ten days collecting rocks and placing them in the labyrinth. Anna had a lot of rocks on her property that we used. The weekend after the election a group of the artists from FIG came out to help finish the project. We were able to celebrate the elections and we had hope for the future. At the Saturday evening campfire on the day the Associated Press called the election for Biden and Harris, we had a burning ritual of drawings I had done of Trump in 2017, which were named *Man of Hate, Pants on Fire, Racist Bigot,* and *Misogynist Bully.*

On Sunday morning we had a ceremony to open the labyrinth. The artists walked the legs of the form and read their artist statements. I read all of the statements of the artists who were not present and the poem "Mulch" by Nilly Gill that is embedded under the rocks. Ted Meyers took pictures of the performance, did interviews after it was over, and edited a video.[17] Joseph Barret brought a drone to get overhead shots of the project and performance.

This project was long and involved and kept me sane and busy during eight months of the lockdown. The labyrinth to me represents the possibility of healing through art

---

[17] "The Walk: A Project by Linda Litteral," by Ted Meyers at Desert Dairy Artist Residency
https://www.youtube.com/watch?v=Ycb2QE9QRzA&t=35s

and is a manifestation of positive change in the world. Viewers who are able to walk the labyrinth can consciously look at the work while meditating on the positive changes they would wish the world to make.

CHAPTER 13

WAYS OF HEALING

There are many different paths to take while traveling my healing spiral. Some are helpful, and some are not. In this last space, I will talk about the specific paths and whether they were healing for me and how. There have been many groups with other survivors over the years, and I have seen people respond individually to different healing modalities. There isn't a right way to do this. We need to trust our inner knowledge by following our feelings to the next step. I found that it has to come from within to be effective. I had to be curious about the therapy to be able to hear it. My intuition was the best indicator of what I should do next to heal.

My unconscious knew when to listen and when to ignore a therapy style. I would brush right past something if it were not the time to try it yet, or I wouldn't even hear it in the first place. Later in my healing process, I would be able to see more clearly and would try those things I ignored in the past. I am always traveling up and down the spiral of my path, moving forward, then stepping back when needed.

I read a lot, especially on healing from childhood sexual abuse. Some of the books I have read more than once. Maybe years later, I would go back and reread them. I would somehow have a thought or feeling that there was something I needed to read in that book, something that I might have ignored earlier but was then ready to explore, and it would pop up in my head. I have included an extensive bibliography of these books. I am not referencing many in this text, but they have all been a part of my healing journey, along with many books I've given to others, or just borrowed from the library. They have all had a part in my understanding of how I was damaged and how I could help myself heal. All of these books had at least one idea or thought that helped illuminate my journey, and some more than others. Some of them brought up *Warning! Warning!* feelings. It was interesting to pick and choose which might have a positive path for me to explore. Some of them just made me angry with their certainty that they knew what I needed to do. I wrote notes and asked questions on the edges of pages as I underlined passages. These messages reveal my thoughts through time when I reread them.

Sometimes I move past that thought and have acquired a greater understanding, so I have new questions.

I find reading to be one of my safest places. I read all the time; I love fantasy, a good mystery, or even a historical novel. Nancy Drew was my first hero. These stories I have read are what kept me from dissolving into pain for much of my life. A good story can distract from guilt and shame. I can escape into another reality and experience how other people see that world. It is a place outside of me that still feels real; it is a relief to live there sometimes. Reading is the first thing I ever did that was positive for me. It helped me to survive my childhood. It helped me see that there were other ways of living life than the one in which I was stuck.

At Christmas when I was two, my mom read us *How the Grinch Stole Christmas* by Dr. Seuss. It was 1957, and it had come out in *Redbook* magazine. She cut the story out of the magazine and used ribbon to put the pages together with a cover she made. My older brother and I sat on her lap in the chair next to the Christmas tree. It was magical. I can still see it happening in my head. I can still feel the fear and awe. *Oh no, he is stealing Christmas; this is horrible.* Then there was the relief when he gave it back. That was the beginning of my love of and need for reading stories. It took me out of myself and into another story.

All through my childhood and teenage years, I was very physically active. I pushed myself in physical activities. I played football with the boys during recess. I was always sent to the principal's office for unladylike things, like jumping off the swing at the highest point, climbing on the barn roof, or hiding at the top of the trees. In the sixties and seventies, there were not many sports in which girls could participate. I tried to do whatever was available: in junior high it was volleyball, track, and cheerleading. In high school, it was gymnastics and cheerleading. The only way I could feel like I was in my body was to push it to the point of pain. I worked out in the weight room; girls were not supposed to do that. I had to get there at 5:00 in the morning before the boys arrived to be able to use the equipment. I think it was my way of protecting myself from the world that was so strange to me. I could be physically strong. Reading was a way to experience the world outside of myself and physical activity was my therapy. These were how I would survive my childhood.

When I was working as a layout designer at a steel fabrication plant in 1977, the town I lived in bought the sculpture *Midsummer Night Tree* by Louise Nevelson. The city paid $75,000 for it. Many were scandalized and angry about public funds being used to buy the work. It polarized the community. Some loved it; others hated it. People were talking about the artwork, many articles were in the paper, and television and radio shows discussed the controversy. It was my first exposure to the power of art, the way people responded to the work, and how they were very vocal about it. I thought about this phenomenon a lot. I think this was my first glimmer that art could be a way of finding my voice. These discussions were a stepping stone to the realization that art can tell your story, and people respond to the art. It took over ten years after that before I was able to take an art class.

Image 13.1   *Healing Art Process #1*

When I was finally able to talk about the sexual abuse, I was 28. I disclosed it to my second husband after we were married; that was when I first went to a talk therapist. As the Navy moved us around the country, I kept finding a new therapist with whom to speak. I think this process was the necessary first step to healing. I needed to be able to find my words around this topic. Words were very difficult, so it was slow going. It was at least ten years before I was able to talk frankly about the abuse at all. Talking about the abuse is still fraught with surprising bursts of uncontrollable emotions, even after 40 years of working on healing. I needed to try to talk about it, even when I couldn't. I think it was an exercise in finding safe spaces and knowing how to recognize them. Some therapists I went to once and never went back. I did not feel safe there. It was an education on how to recognize that safe person or place. For a long time, no one and nowhere was safe.

I discovered clay in South Carolina. I kept being refused for design and drafting jobs. When I went to apply, I repeatedly heard, "We do not hire women in this department." It was 1988. The patriarchy was hard at work. I decided to learn how to work with porcelain. I had seen some earrings made with it and thought it looked like fun. I had never tried any art before that. I didn't make any earrings, but the instructor, Duke Ready, saw something in what I made and invited me to join his sculpture class. That was the beginning of a growing need to express myself visually, and eventually it was the door that allowed me to start looking at more ways to heal. The first piece I did was an anteater. He did not want us to look at any images, but to make it from our minds. I chose the first animal I came to in the dictionary. It ended up being a vaguely male figure on hands and knees with a protruding nose that was faintly penile, a very strange form, but Duke's response when he saw it the first time was that it made his hairs stand on end. From his view, he said it seemed to be an atavistic response to fear. This was another indicator of the power of visual imagery.

When we moved to Maine in 1989, I began attending the University of New Hampshire. They did not have a ceramics department, but they had an excellent classical art program. My drawing classes began here. I found a new therapist after talking to several. The women's studies department allowed me to do a graduate class of my own design, researching alternative healing modalities for healing sexual abuse. I talked to many different people, tried some things myself, and then wrote about them. This was also when I began unraveling and recognizing that I was losing time. The way the abused mind takes over and does not allow conscious understanding is insidious. It took some time to recognize it was happening. I felt like I was going crazy. This is when I went into the hospital and tried different healing modalities. We did expressive body exercises, art therapy, talk therapy, writing exercises, and yelling exercises; I explored them all.

Some of them I could not even do. Yelling? No way. Make a loud sound? Forget it. The body exercises exposed that I was frozen in place, allowing myself very little movement. I was unable to do anything that would bring attention to myself. The writing showed more scribbles than words. I think I regressed to a very young place while trying to do these things. At this time, art therapy was the only thing that felt safe enough to do. I didn't have to show anyone. I would draw in my room and keep those drawings for myself. I did the art therapy exercises in a therapy session, but not as freely as when by myself. I think this process of creative thinking, trying to show what my feelings were on paper, was what allowed me to begin my healing journey. The emotions were not as frightening on paper as they were inside me. I looked at them instead of closing down, which was my usual reaction to strong emotions. I stayed present when I drew feelings but not when I felt them.

Image 13.2   *Healing Art Process #2*

Words are powerful. I think the labels we are given have an effect on how we perceive ourselves. It's important to question whether we agree with a label or title we are given, especially for sexual abuse survivors. The diagnoses I received at times made me question the entire mental health apparatus. I don't think sexual abuse survivors are mentally ill. We are damaged, as if we had been hit by a car. Someone damaged our psyche. A virus or cancer did not attack our body. In my opinion, the difference here is huge. The way we see ourselves is different. If I had cancer, I would get treatment or not. I would wonder what had caused it: air, asbestos, diet, etc. If I had schizophrenia, I would wonder if it was genetic. Sexual abuse is a direct violent attack on my person by another person. It is a different experience entirely. My suggestion—look at the words that have been applied to you from every angle and decide if they feel right, whatever your story is. Maybe you have schizophrenia and sexual abuse is also part of your experience. Question any diagnosis. Push to understand. Do not let anyone's words define you. She was a victim; I am a survivor. One is helpless; the other is taking control. Label yourself with words that empower you.

Image 13.3   *Healing Art Process #3*

I found a massage therapist who had developed a modality she called *Safe Touch*. She was an incest survivor and wanted to help others be present in their bodies. The first time I went to see her, she touched my left ankle, and she was physically pushed back from the table by the amount of electrical energy I released. She said this was normal in abuse survivors as we tend to store the trauma in our bodies. It was a bizarre feeling. I do think it released some of the pain I had been holding for about 35 years at that point.

Church counseling was one of the things that I researched at this time. This was the least helpful thing I considered. It was actually harmful. They stressed how I had to give the abuse to God. That *He* would heal me. I found it very difficult to comprehend. My grandfather, the person who abused me, went to church when he remarried. I vaguely remember him telling me that God felt what he did was okay.

Everything I read in the Bible felt like it was trying to control me in the same way he did. All the sermons I heard were about how men must guide women and children. I don't buy it. I don't believe there is some white man up in heaven telling us what the right thing is to do. I see that as another patriarchal construct, made up to control women and children especially, but everyone is included. It is a male fantasy that the majority of the world follows. It doesn't matter which religion you observe; they all have similar tropes designed to keep women and children in check. I feel slightly sick to my stomach when I read a book about an abuse survivor who uses God as her healing modality, and there are many. I think they are not really healed, just under control. This control hides the underlying damage, so the damage is not allowed to be felt and dealt with. Abuse is pushed down and you live in a pretend reality where healing is not achieved. It seems to me it's another way of hiding what has happened and saying it's okay. You are silenced again. I find it is a commentary on the fear that men have of women.

The Art for Healing was an exhibition curated by Judy Wilbur-Albertson that I had art in—this was a powerful healing moment in 1990. It was an international show with over a hundred artists participating. The art exposed the artists' experiences with sexual abuse, spousal abuse, and other traumas. I felt a part of something. I was no longer alone in my pain. I could see the other artists' pain in their work. Understanding that there were others like me out there was easier to accept through their art than through words. I could feel my own emotions while I was looking at their art. I also spent the two weeks of the show volunteering as a docent, and the process of seeing others respond to the work was cathartic. I could see my reactions to the art repeated over and over in others. It was an exposé of things I had kept hidden since the abuse occurred. The responses to the art were normal. Wow, what a blast of understanding. I was not abnormal or weird. I was the same as other survivors.

Trauma's emotions were visible in the art. Viewers cried, cringed, and responded strongly to what they saw. What had to be hidden as a victim suddenly was exposed. The visceral response to the art was real. When the abuse was being perpetrated, I could not respond. Emotions were not allowed. I could not scream, I could not run, and I could not express any of the horror and fear, the total shock of *what the fuck is this?* I had no questions to ask anyone about something I did not understand. Suddenly, viewing the art, I felt those emotions I wasn't allowed to feel in the past. Others visually exposed the same feelings I experienced from my trauma. It was the first place that was safe enough actually to experience the emotions that were buried for so long. I did not run screaming, but was able to feel. This was new.

It also was the impetus for continuing to make art about sexual abuse. It validated what I was thinking and feeling about making art. It showed me that this was another way to talk about it. Communicating the emotions, pain, and history through art was a powerful force for healing. The expression of my experience was important. It connected me to others like me.

I found cognitive therapy (CBT) to be useless for me. I knew all the answers; I didn't discover anything helpful. Psychoanalysis was also strange and intrusive, not helpful for me to understand myself. The therapists who encouraged me to be with my feelings, to remember at my pace, and to work on what came up in the moment had the most positive results, when there was no agenda to follow. I had to come to understand myself at my own pace and remember when I needed to, not when someone asked me to talk about certain aspects of the abuse. The therapists who were helpful provided the safe places I needed. Suz Trolinger, a therapist within the Naval Medical Community, was amazing. I saw her for over ten years until she retired. She allowed me to find understanding and pushed me when I needed it.

Image 13.4   *Healing Art Process #5*

She introduced me to other healing modalities. Eye Movement Desensitization and Reprocessing (EMDR) was one process Suz suggested. It uses eye movements to redirect a traumatic memory and reprocess it in a different way. The EMDR specialist decided I was not a good candidate for that when she interviewed me. I don't remember why. It has been shown in studies to be helpful for PTSD. They both felt that art, music, and dance were healthy ways for me to find my feelings.

Acupuncture is another method I have used over the years. It is helpful in unblocking the energy pathways throughout my body. I have used it mostly for pain control instead of painkillers. It is effective and helpful. I would have used it more to directly address my abuse issues if it had been covered by my insurance.

I have been doing sacral cranial therapy for about fifteen years. It addresses the rhythmic system that is at the core of our physiology. It is a gentle, intuitive technique that uses slight pressure on the cranial bones and the sacral area of the body. I find it the most helpful of all the body-memory therapies. It also allows me to remember at my pace. It is more about body memories that I recover, about feeling something physically that has been hidden since the abuse. It can be very intense. One of the sessions involved the therapist moving a block inside my body from my pelvis area up and out through my head. I could feel a hard ball traveling up my spine, through my stomach and throat, almost choking me, feeling hard and cold, moving through my body until it was released. It was very real, as if an actual ball was enclosed in my body. There was a tremendous sense of loss and relief when it went out through the top of my head. It was like a pop of energy was released. I have had many similar experiences. These sessions always exhaust me; I sleep a lot after them. I have seen several different practitioners, and like the talk therapists, some are better than others, or I can respond to certain people better than others; I am not sure which.

I have had many different massage therapists. Again, some are better than others. I tend to stick with female practitioners, as they feel safer, but I have had male therapists at times when it felt important to push at and try to expand my safe-place feelings. I do think it is essential for us to remember how to feel in our bodies. That's one of the first things damaged when we are sexually abused. We do not feel safe in our bodies, so we discontinue feeling there; at least, I did. Recovering mindfulness in my body was a key component in my healing. The ability to feel sensations in my body has been recovered very slowly and over time. I am still healing this part that was damaged.

I spoke with a sex therapist once and I have not returned to that topic yet. I don't know if I ever will. It was too overwhelming and terrifying to ponder at that time. I almost ran from that therapy session.

Sex itself has always been problematic. I went without for many years. I was very promiscuous, dangerously so for some periods. Within marriage, sex kind of works. A lot of the time I thought about other things while it was going on. I can sometimes be present as it is happening. Sometimes a smell will set me off and I have to stop, or a physical flashback will come through, and again, I have to stop. It is still a topic I am uncomfortable talking about and I avoid it most of the time. Friends will talk about it, laughing and commenting, and I can't seem to participate. Healing is still happening around the idea of sex.

I joined Toastmasters in 2010, an international organization that teaches people how to negotiate public speaking. They have guidebooks for different kinds of public speaking that you develop topics for and practice at the meetings. I participated in this organization for over three years. Every Friday morning at seven, I would practice how to speak. I learned how to prepare for a presentation. It was a smaller group than most of the Toastmasters chapters, with about twelve people, many of whom had been doing it for years. There was a lot of experience in helping others enhance their speaking abilities. Everyone was supportive and wanted me to improve. It was very helpful in refining my ability to think in the moment and speak with others or to speak in front of a group. When I began, I could barely speak. I needed to read my presentations, and it was difficult. I progressed over time. I would recommend this organization to anyone; just remember that different chapters are run differently. Choose the one most helpful to you. I would not have been able to participate and continue in some of the other chapters I visited when I was deciding whether to join. There were too many people in some of the groups. Some were not as gentle about corrections or as accepting of my story as the group I eventually joined.

Image 13.5   *Healing Art Process #6*

Breathing is also a problem. I have taken harmonica lessons to try to breathe better. I have tried shamanic breathwork and other attempts to learn how to breathe normally. All my life, I have breathed very shallowly. It is difficult for me to take a deep breath, as it feels wrong. It still takes a conscious effort for me to breathe deeply. I held my breath a lot during the abuse. It was one of the ways I was able to stay silent and still. I would take shallow breaths so my response could not reach the surface. At different times during my day, I still find myself holding my breath frequently.

Tai Chi Qigong has been helpful with learning to breathe more normally and more deeply. It is a process where you breathe with the movements, and the breathing seems more natural within those steps. In one class I took, the instructor had a DVD by Chris Enders that I bought and continue to use—it has the breathing instructions written under the exercise. It helps me remember to breathe and consciously choose to breathe. There are movements where breath is the important part of the exercise. These are the best exercises.

I have done yoga periodically throughout my life. At times I take classes, and then I don't for a while. It is sporadic. Then I feel the need to do it again and find another class. This is another therapy that has helped me to be present with my body. It demands that I pay attention to my body as I hold the poses. Am I doing it correctly? Am I stretching too much, or not enough? Breathing is also talked about in the movements. I highly recommend it as a way to get in touch with feeling your body. You have to be in the moment and mindful of what your body is doing. It was helpful for me.

Dance was another way I was able to feel my body. I took classes as a child, not as an adult, but I was always on the dance floor when I was out and about with groups of people. It was also a way that allowed me to be in large groups of people. I am uncomfortable in crowds. I feel hemmed in, controlled in space by people. It is not a good feeling. Dance allowed me to be present in crowds and not be so uncomfortable.

Sound therapies have been a large part of my life for the last 20 years. I found Dr. Jeffery Thompson's music, especially his *Creative Mind System, Healing Mind System, Awakened Mind System,* and *Brainwave Symphony*, to be calming and yet stimulating. I crave the mental calm I have when I listen. I also found the music helpful in some of my classes when I was teaching. When the students were agitated and distracted, I would play his music and watch them get into their own heads and focus on their artwork more positively. It is an obvious change in behavior based on sound.

I also listen to the Solfeggio frequencies. I read about Hildegard of Bingen, a nun from the 1100s who had written soaring melodies that pushed the edges of the Gregorian chants of the day, which led me to the Solfeggio frequencies. I especially like one that is called *Seven Chakra Healing,* by Spiritual Moment, which moves through the frequencies in conjunction with the chakras. I also like *All 9 Solfeggio Frequencies* by Miracle Tones. They are calming and beautiful.

I find that I can move into my creative mind more quickly with the different sound therapies I have described here. I focus faster on what I am working on and can work longer with focus when listening. I always have something like the above-mentioned music on in my studio while working. Research has shown that these types of music are healing in and of themselves.

Labyrinths are another place of healing for me. I have walked many different public and private ones. I have constructed a small one in my flower garden. In Chapter 12, I wrote about the one I created at Dairy Desert Artist Residency in 29 Palms. I consider it a public art piece. It is a form of physical meditation as you walk a labyrinth's path. It can just be about the walk or you can enter with an intention to work on during the movement. I find it freeing and clearing to do a labyrinth walk and meditation. I visit one periodically to do this. If you do a search, you may find a public labyrinth in your area, or you can build your own.

Another modality I did is called the Healing Touch Program, an energy-healing therapy. My therapist Sue used her hands to restore balance to my energy field. She told me that by clearing and balancing my energy system, I would be in a position to allow my internal healing system to work more efficiently. It was a calming and fluid type of therapy; she held her hands over different areas of my body and cleared that energy area. I could feel the energy pool in that area, and I felt lighter as the therapy went on.

Reiki and theta healing were other therapies I tried. Reiki is an ancient Japanese technique that uses the body's energies and tries to clear and realign the body's energetic system. Theta therapy uses the theta brainwave to allow communication between the body and the mind and to enhance natural healing within the self. These are both interesting; I always felt clearer after a session. They both promote your inner healing, allowing you to be part of the healing process. Theta brainwaves are thought to occur when your brain is in a meditative process.

Meditation is also something I practice. It is a difficult yet satisfying journey. It calms and allows a deeper understanding within myself. Whenever I am having a hard time focusing or staying present, I try to do at least 30 minutes of meditation, and it always brings me back into myself at some level. It is sometimes more successful than others. Quiet helps for me. Being alone with myself and trying to see within is sometimes illuminating. There are many different types of meditation styles out there. I tried several different methods until I felt comfortable with the process.

Creative visualization has been one of the most successful styles of meditation for me. Shakti Gawain has a book called *Creative Visualization* that is excellent and a CD that is very helpful in moving you through the exercises in the book. There are many other books about this topic if you want to explore it further. The first time I tried this was around 1989. I was at the University of New Hampshire and sitting outside a classroom waiting for my class to start. I had a book with creative visualization exercises, so I tried one. I was amazed at where it took me. I don't have the book anymore and don't remember the name, so I can't share it with you. It was a simple exercise though: close your eyes, see a road, follow that road, and see where it takes you. Then see where you can make it go. Visualize the route in your head and watch what comes up. Can you go to a specific place? Can you make up a new place? What do you see on the journey?

Another thing I use as a healing entity is scent. I have found that smells can trigger a flashback. Odors can make me uncomfortable and lost in memory. I have been using aromatherapy products that are calming and give me a sense of knowing where I am in space. Young Living has products formulated to address sexual abuse and trauma. *Sara*, *White Angelica*, and *Release* are the mixtures I use the most. I find them to be a way to make my space feel safer.

My latest therapist Dr. Robert Bray and his approach using energy psychology have created a space for my continued healing. His use of Thought Field Therapy techniques is critical to keeping me grounded and thinking. It allows me to move back from the chaotic emotions that come up when we are working in session and anytime I am triggered. The customized tapping sequences he has given me for use at home help me to help myself stay in the moment. The tapping keeps me from spiraling back into the emotions from the past and stay in the present. I would recommend his process to anyone dealing with sexual trauma or any form of violence.[18] Explore for yourself how to use this easy, safe way to stay in the moment and address the past.[19]

Healing is an ongoing and memorable journey. The spiral I am on moves me back and forth in many directions whenever I am healed enough to move to the next step. I address what is relevant when I need to. Sometimes I need to work on shame, other times on being in my body, or breathing, etc. Things pop up and I deal with them in that moment. Healing is not a straight line for me. I jump around to the parts of me that have been damaged. Healing is a process of learning about myself and being kind to myself, allowing that I deserve to be healed, understanding that my black space was what saved me as a child, and reminding me to be gentle with myself when I go back there. I negotiate with the behavior and let it know it is no longer needed as I can protect myself now.

My younger self still jumps up and says *No, no, no. Do not do that. It is not safe.* Again, I have to be gentle with her and let her know that I am strong enough now to keep both of us safe. Her feelings do not have to overpower me in the present. I need to teach her how to feel safe within me.

The negative voices that are in my head call me names, the voices of all the people in my life who have been damaging to me—my grandpa Jerome; my first-grade teacher, Mrs. White; my first husband, Doug; and others—they all damaged my younger self and programmed me to feel less than, and those results need to be healed. It is sad to think about how many people have had a negative effect on my development. Paying

---

[18] Thought Field Therapy techniques and other forms of energy psychology are well-researched. More information is available at Association for Comprehensive Energy Psychology resource page at https://www.energypsych.org/researchdb8c71b7#ResearchQuickFacts

[19] For a video to see a standard tapping technique ag to https://rlbray.com/services/thought-field-therapy/

attention to those voices and addressing how wrong they are in the moment has helped my self-esteem and self-worth. By talking back and saying *No, I am not stupid*, I take more control over how I feel and negotiate the world.

I call this "the itty, bitty, shitty committee." I heard this somewhere, and it has become my mantra to the voices. "You are not correct, you do not get to call me names in my head, what you say is not what I am." Even though I hear those voices in my voice, I know it is old programming from the abuse and my childhood or from my abusive marriage. I internalized the messages so much that they are now in my voice rather than in the voices of the people who first said them to me. The process of taking away their power is always to talk back and tell them they are wrong and that what they say is not true.

I described earlier a performance piece I developed around the topics of this book with Nikki Dunnan, a dancer and choreographer who works at Art Produce in San Diego. She teaches dance at local schools and performs in the community. I am terrified and excited by the process. This mode of communication is very different than others I have done in the past. I find it to be healing for me to learn how to expose sexual abuse with my body movements. There are connections being made between my body and my memories throughout the process.[20]

The teaching process has also been very healing for me. Teaching art at Las Colinas Detention Center has been amazing. I watch these women, many who have been sexually abused themselves, find their personal voice through drawing. I can see them get stronger internally and face their fears and grow. I watch their self-esteem grow as they learn to draw. I can see them visually voice many of their fears and past traumas, while moving forward and drawing a different future for themselves. I think every jail, prison, and detention facility should have a resident artist who helps the people incarcerated there to find their voices, helping them work through things creatively without judgement.

As I have said, the healing process is continual for sexual abuse survivors. We heal something, move on in our lives, and then need to heal the next thing. I have found that I need to be intense about healing for a certain amount of time, and then rest from it for a while to let the healing become integrated into my being and change my behavior over time. I keep going back, healing more and trying to help others heal.

As a culture we need to address the way words are used to describe women and children who have been sexually assaulted. Although I mentioned this earlier, it bears repeating. Words are powerful and they can convey a perception that is widespread and false. The medical community needs to consider how they label people who have experienced trauma. The way they diagnose and tell us what is wrong with us is a re-

---

[20] It is available to watch on my YouTube channel at
https://www.youtube.com/@lindalitteral2167

traumatization of the abuse. This holds true I think for soldiers who have experienced wartime traumas also. Buck up and soldier on; it is your fault that you are having problems because you are not strong enough to handle the action. Minimizing the trauma is a negative approach that never works.

The perceptions we have of ourselves after those diagnoses are negative. I do not think I have mental illness issues, even though I have been diagnosed as such; I have a brain that has been damaged by trauma and needs to be healed. This is a totally different way to think about the process of healing and how I perceive myself. While most of society thinks that once you have a mental illness, you have that illness forever, I think that we can heal from trauma. While this healing process has been a lifelong exercise for me, I think that if we begin to look at abuse more clearly, to talk about it and its effects more freely, and start the healing process at a younger age, there is hope for more positive outcomes for survivors. Rather than negating their experience with words, we should embrace and honor them as survivors of something horrific. Society has a negative view of mental illness or the effects of trauma in any of its forms. This judgmental view compounds the difficulty in healing. There should not be such a negative belief system around people suffering from mental illness, or trauma—it's just something that is. The worldview of these issues is part of the problem. It keeps people from going for help when they need to. There is nothing wrong with suffering from mental illness; it is just something that is part of the human condition.

I think the entire false-memory syndrome, developed by a couple who were accused of abuse by their daughter, has been invented and perpetuated by the society that allows the abuse to occur, the culture that has almost always blamed the victim. This culture uses words to paint the victim as wrong when they do speak up. When abuse is talked about and exposed, there is a huge backlash mechanism that raises its ugly head and minimizes what was done to the victim. The victim is guilty, whether of wearing the wrong thing, of being at the wrong place, of being seductive, or of lying. Apparently, perpetrators have no control over their actions and are the victims of their desires when they are confronted with a lovely child or a girl in a short skirt. This is pathetic.

All of the processes I talk about here have been helpful in my healing. It may have just taught me something, or moved me forward in some way. Everything enlightened me in some way. There were some things that were more effective for me and pushed me along in a dramatic way. I think we all have to just keep looking for and at what might be helpful. When new information is put out into the world, we owe it to ourselves to look at it and see if it might help. Use what works, and disregard what does not resonate with you.

I did another installation at *Mojaveland,* an interactive art experience in 29 Palms, California. Artists designed different miniature golf holes and other permanent artworks. My piece there is called *Wind Whispers* — it is a series of kinetic sculptures that hang from a preexisting old structure. They are constructed of pinch pots that are hanging with jewelry wire. The pots weave and wave in the wind. There is almost always some kind of wind in the Mojave so they move in many different patterns depending on the strength of that wind. It is a meditative piece; to watch the swaying of the forms is to clear and cleanse my mind. It is peaceful.[21]

Image 13.6 *Wind Whispers*

The pots swaying in the wind can be mesmerizing and allow you to step away from everyday difficulties for a bit of time. A healing experience through art.

---

[21] You can see the pinch pots in motion on my Instagram/@lindalitteralartist, or on YouTube at https://youtu.be/MudjAL73AxI. You can visit the website http://www.mojaveland.com for more information.

POEM
"WHAT"

Black full of color
Black to not see
Black to hide and be safe
Black mind overreaching all
My heart shivers
My mind hides
Energy flows over my skin
I am scared
Drawing space
Drawing time
Drawing experience
Drawing Pain
Creativity soothes
Creativity exposes
Creativity explores
Creativity balances
Sexual trauma
Damages all
It will take all
To heal

Image 0.4   *What*   Image 0.5   *What, detail*

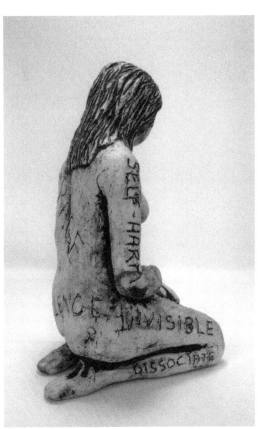

Image 0.6   *What, detail*

Image 0.7   *What, detail*

EPILOGUE

I would like to say to you, *Do Not Invalidate Your Experience*. We all have a story, and the way we react to it is our own. Every child's trauma as they perceived it is unique. We all respond to abuse differently. We all develop coping mechanisms that are from our subconscious and again are our own. Every way we developed to survive is powerful and important and our own. We all experience our stories and respond to them in a unique way.

Certain things trigger me that might not trigger you, and vice versa. There is not a ruler that measures how this was more horrible than that. It is all wrong and just needs to be survived.

Honor your survival.

Within this jumble of words and images, I hope that you have found one thing that resonated with you and helped you see the world or yourself in a new and interesting way. Thank you for looking and reading.

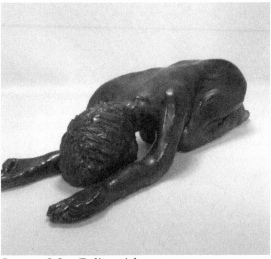

Image 0.8   *Relinquish*

ABOUT THE AUTHOR

Linda Litteral is a multi-faceted artist working alternately with ceramics, bronze cast and clay sculpture, oil and acrylic paint on canvas, pen and pencil on paper, wood, and three-dimensional mixed media sculpture. Linda earned her MFA from San Diego State University. Her thesis was an exploration of art as a way to expose and heal childhood abuse of which she is a survivor. Her past teaching experience includes SDSU, Mesa, Miramar, Grossmont, and Southwestern Colleges.

She has taught art healing classes to inmates at Las Colinas Detention Center and Robert J. Donovan Correctional Facility. Linda also teaches private classes on art and healing. Recently, she facilitated a similar class at New York City's prestigious Bluestockings Cooperative Bookstore. She is a member of Allied Craftsman and is director of the Feminist Image Group (FIG).

Her work has been seen extensively in Greater San Diego, around the US, and is included in the collections of Museu Brasileira De Escultura (The Brazil Museum of Culture) in Sao Paulo, Brazil, and Jingdezhen Ceramic Institute in Jingdzhen, China. Litteral curated the FIG show, *Don't Shut Up!* at City College. She travelled to New York City to represent the artists and their movement at Ceres Gallery. She has shown her work at Grafiska Sallskapet and Krogen Amerika in Sweden. Litteral was also chosen for and attended a coveted two-month residency at Centre Pompadour in France for women artists creating social change through their art in 2018.

As an artist, she is passionate about making the world a safer place for women and children. She uses her art to educate, heal viewers, and as an activist statement about sexual abuse. Her classes help people of all ages open to healing themselves and their communities.

BIBLIOGRAPHY

Abramson, Edward. *Art as Healing.* London: Coventure Ltd., 1984.

Abramson, Tania Love. *Shame and the Eternal Abyss.* Joshua Tree, CA: Asylum 4 Renegades Press, 2017.

Ainscough, Carolyn, and Kay Toon. *Surviving Childhood Sexual Abuse.* New York: Fisher Books, 2000.

Allender, Dr. Dan B. *The Wounded Heart: Hope for Adult Victims of Childhood Sexual Abuse.* Colorado Springs: Navpress, 1995.

Andrews, Ted. *The Healer's Manual: A Beginner's Guide to Energy Therapies.* St Paul: Llewellyn Publications, 1993.

Arnheim, Rudolf. *Visual Thinking.* Berkeley: University of California Press, 1969.

Arnheim, Rudolf. *The Power of the Center: A Study of Composition in the Visual Arts.* Berkeley: University of California Press, 1988.

Baldwin, MSSW, Martha. *Beyond Victim.* Moore Haven, FL: Rainbow Books, 1988.

Baker, Christine D. *Female Survivors of Sexual Abuse.* New York: Tayler and Francis, Inc., 2002.

Bass, Ellen, and Laura Davis. *The Courage to Heal.* New York: Harper & Row Publishers, Inc., 1988.

Bass, Ellen, and Louise Thornton. *I Never Told Anyone: Writings by Women Survivors of Child Sexual Abuse.* New York: Harper & Row Publishers, Inc., 1983.

Bender, Gretchen, Tania Bruguera, Lygia Clark, and Christine Hohenbüchler. *Pulse: Art, Healing, and Transformation.* Boston: The Institute of Contemporary Art, 2003.

Black, Claudia. *It's Never Too Late to Have a Happy Childhood.* New York: Ballantine Books, 1989.

Blume, Sue E. *Secret Survivors: Uncovering Incest and Its Aftereffects in Women.* New York: John Wiley and Sons, 1990.

Bray, Dr. Robert. *Open Wounds: Heal Traumatic Stress Now.* Fremont, CA: Robertson Publishing, 2008.

Bromley, Nicole Braddock. *Hush.* Chicago: Moody Publishers, 2007.

Bronson, Catherine. *Growing Through the Pain: The Incest Survivor's Companion*. Park Ridge, IL: Prentiss Hall Press, 1989.

Brooks, Ph.D., Kathleen. *Radical Integrity*. San Diego: Self Published, 2011.

Broude, Norma, and Mary D. Garrard. *The Power of Feminist Art*. New York: Henry N. Abrams, Inc., 1993.

Brown, Abigail. *And Don't Tell Anyone*. St Cloud, MN: North Star Press of St. Cloud, 1997.

Capacchione, Ph.D., Lucia. *The Art of Emotional Healing*. Boston: Shambala Publications, Inc., 2001.

Carey, Lois. *Expressive and Creative Arts Methods for Trauma Survivors*. London: Jessica Kingsley Publishers, 2006.

Chopra, M.C. Deepak. *Quantum Healing*. New York: Bantam Books, 1989.

Clancey, Ph.D., Susan A. *The Trauma Myth*. New York: Basic Books, 2009.

Cohen, Barry M., Mary-Michola Barnes, and Anita B. Rankin. *Managing Traumatic Stress Through Art: Drawing from the Center*. Lutherville, MD: The Sidran Press, 1995.

Costin, Lela B., Howard Jacob Karger, and David Stoesz. *The Politics of Child Abuse in America*. New York: Oxford University Press, 1996.

Cross, Jen. *Writing Ourselves Whole: Using the Power of Your Own Creativity to Recover and Heal from Sexual Trauma*. Coral Gables, FL: Mango Publishing, 2017.

Cross, Jen. *Write to Restore: A Step-by-Step Creative Writing Journal for Survivors of Sexual Trauma*. Coral Gables, FL: Mango Publishing, 2019.

Curtis, Amy Stacey. *Women, Trauma, & Visual Expression*. Portland, ME: WTVE, 2005.

Damasio, Antonio. *The Feeling of What Happens: Body and Emotions in the Making of Consciousness*. New York: Houghton Mifflin Harcourt Publishing Company, 1999.

Davis, Laura. *The Courage to Heal Workbook*. New York: Harper and Row Publishers, 1990.

Davis, Laura. *Allies in Healing*. New York: Harper Collins, 1991.

DeSalvo, Louise. *Virginia Woolf*. Boston: Beacon Press, 1989.

Duncan, Karen A. *Healing from the Trauma of Childhood Sexual Abuse: The Journey for Women*. Westport, CT: Praeger Publishers, 2004.

Edelman, Murray. *From Art to Politics: How Artistic Creations Shape Political Conceptions*. Chicago: The University of Chicago Press, 1995.

Edwards, Betty. *Drawing on the Right Side of the Brain*. London: Penguin Books, 1979.

Edwards, Betty. *Drawing on the Artist Within*. New York: Simon and Schuster, 1986.

Elbrecht, Cornelia. *Healing Trauma with Guided Drawing*. Berkeley: North Atlantic Books, 2018.

Ferrara, Felicia F. *Childhood Sexual Abuse*. Pacific Grove: Brooks/Cole, 2002.

Fezler, Ph.D., William. *Creative Imagery*. New York: Simon and Schuster, 1989.

Fezler, Ph.D., William. *Imagery for Healing, Knowledge and Power*, 1990.

Finkelhor, David. *Child Sexual Abuse*. New York: The Free Press, 1984.

Finkelhor, David, and Associates. *A Sourcebook on Childhood Sexual Abuse.* Beverly Hills: Sage Publications, 1986.

Finney, J.D., MSW, Lynne D. *Reach for the Rainbow.* New York: Perigee Press, 1990.

Forward, Dr. Susan, and Craig Buck. *Betrayal of Innocence.* New York: Penguin Books, 1978.

Fraser, Sylvia. *My Father's House: A Memoir of Incest and of Healing.* New York: Harper and Row, 1987.

French, Marilyn. *The War Against Women.* New York: Ballantine Books, 1992.

French, Stanley B., Wanda Teays, and Laura M. Purdy. *Violence Against Women.* Ithaca: Cornell University Press, 1998.

Fryd, Vivien Green. *Against Our Will.* University Park, PA: Penn State University Press, 2019.

Furth, Gregg M. *The Secret World of Drawing.* Boston: Sigo Press, 1988.

Gabriel, Orion Marie. *Going Sane.* Independently Published, 2015.

Gabriel, Orion Marie. *A Spectacular Dawn.* Independently Published, 2015.

Gabriel, Orion Marie. *The White House.* Independently Published, 2015.

Ganim, Barbara. *Art & Healing: Using Expressive Art to Heal Your Body, Mind, and Spirit.* Brattleboro, VT: Echo Point Books & Media, 1999.

Gaspard, Bridgit Dengel. *The Final 8th.* Novato, CA: New World Library, 2020.

Gawain, Shakti. *Creative Visualization.* Novato, CA: New World Library, 1995.

Gawain, Shakti. *The Creative Visualization Workbook.* Novato, CA: New World Library, 1995.

Gil, Ph.D., Eliana. *Outgrowing the Pain.* New York: Dell Publishing, 1983.

Gil, Ph.D., Eliana. *Helping Abused and Traumatized Children.* New York: The Guilford Press, 2006.

Glaser, Danya, and Stephen Frosh. *Child Sexual Abuse.* London: Macmillan Education Ltd., 1988.

Grant, Rachel. *Beyond Surviving: The Final Stage in Recovery from Sexual Abuse,* Bloomington, IN: iUniverse, 2012.

Hegstrom, Ph.D., Paul. *Broken Children, Grown-Up Pain.* Kansas City, MO: Beacon Hill Press, 2001.

Henderson, Helene. *Domestic Violence and Child Abuse Sourcebook.* Detroit: Omnigraphics, 2000.

Henley, David. *Clayworks in Art Therapy: Plying the Sacred Circle.* London: Jessica Kingsley Publishers, 2002.

Herman, M.D., Judith. *Trauma and Recovery.* New York: Basic Books, 1992.

hooks, bell. *Art on My Mind: Visual Politics.* New York: The New Press, 1995.

Jacobs, Janet Liebman. *Victimized Daughters: Incest and the Development of the Female Self.* New York: Routledge, 1994.

Jones, MA, LMFT, Sharyn Higdon. *Healing Steps.* San Jose, CA: Inner Journey Publishing, 2018.

Kaplan, Frances F. *Art Therapy and Social Action.* London: Jessica Kingsley Publishers, 2007.

Kincaid, James R. *Erotic Innocence: The Culture of Child Molesting.* London: Duke University Press, 1998.

Kinnear, Karen L. *Childhood Sexual Abuse.* Santa Barbara: ABC-CLIO, Inc., 2007.

Koplewicz, Harold S., and Robin F. Goodman. *Childhood Revealed, Art Expressing Pain, Discovery and Hope.* New York: Harry N. Abrams, Inc., 1999.

Langer, Ellen J. *Mindfulness.* Reading: Addison-Wesley Publishing Company, Inc., 1989.

Leiderman, M.D., Paul C., and Farideh H. Rezai, Ph.D. *Healing the Wounds of Abuse.* San Diego: Leiderman and Rezai Publications, 1991.

Lerner, Ph.D., Harriet Goldhor. *The Dance of Anger.* New York: Harper and Row, 1985.

Lerner, Ph.D., Harriet Goldhor. *Women in Therapy.* New York: Harper and Row, 1989.

Levenkron, Steven. *Stolen Tomorrows.* New York: W. W. Norton & Company, Inc., 2007.

Levine, Ph.D., Peter A. *Healing Trauma,* Boulder: Sounds True, 2008.

Levine, Ph.D., Peter A., and Maggie Kline, MS, MFT. *Trauma Through a Child's Eye.* Berkeley: North Atlantic Press, 2007.

Lumen, Louise. *Descent and Return.* Ashville, NC: Chiron Publishing, 2017.

Lyshak-Stelzer, Francie. *The Secret: Art & Healing from Sexual Abuse.* Brandon, VT: Safer Society Press, 1999.

Marberry, Sara O., and Laurie Zagon. *The Power of Color.* New York: John Wiley and Sons, Inc., 1995.

Marie, Gabriel Orion, *The White House: Recovery from Incest Through Painting My Story (Book One),* ePubconversions.com, Wise Media Group, 2012.

Marie, Gabriel Orion, *Going Sane: Recovery from Incest Through Painting My Story (Book Two),* ePubconversions.com, Wise Media Group, 2012.

Marie, Gabriel Orion, *The Spectacular Dawn: Recovery from Incest Through Painting My Story (Book Three),* ePubconversions.com, Wise Media Group, 2012.

McKinnon, Marjorie. *Repair Your Life.* Ann Arbor: Loving Healing Press, 2008.

McLaren, Karla. *Rebuilding the Garden: Healing the Spiritual Wounds of Childhood Sexual Assault.* Columbia, CA: Laughing Tree Press, 1997.

McMurray, Madeline. *Illuminations: The Healing Image.* Berkeley: Wingbow Press, 1988.

McNiff, Shaun. *Art as Medicine.* Boston: Shambala Publications, Inc., 1992.

McNiff, Shaun. *Art Heals: How Creativity Heals the Soul.* Boston: Shambala Publications, Inc., 2004.

Miller, Alice. *The Drama of the Gifted Child,* New York: Basic Books, 1981.

Miller, Alice. *For Your Own Good: Hidden Cruelty in Child-rearing and the Roots of Violence.* Toronto: Collins Publishers, 1983.

Miller, Alice. *Thou Shalt Not Be Aware: Society's Betrayal of the Child.* New York: Penguin, Inc., 1986.

Miller, Alice. *Breaking Down the Wall of Silence.* New York: Meridian, 1993.

Miller, Alice. *Pictures of a Childhood.* New York: Meridian, 1995.

Miller, Alice. *Banished Knowledge: Facing Childhood Injuries.* New York: Bantam, Doubleday, Dell Publishing Group, Inc., 1999.

Miller, Alice. *The Untouched Key. Tracing Childhood Trauma in Creativity and Destructiveness.* New York: Bantam, Doubleday, Dell Publishing Group, 2000.

Miller, Alice. *The Truth Will Set You Free: Overcoming Emotional Blindness and Finding Your True Adult Self.* New York: Basic Books, 2001.

Miller, Alice. *The Body Never Lies,* New York: W. W. Norton & Company, Inc. 2004.

Mullinar, Liz. *Heal for Life.* Broadmeadow, NSW: Heal for Life Foundation, 2020.

Murdock, Maureen. *Spinning Inwards.* Boston: Shambhala Publications, Inc., 1987.

Naparstek, Belleruth. *Invisible Heroes: Survivors of Trauma and How They Heal.* New York: Random House, Inc., 2004.

Nightingale, Florence. *Notes on Nursing: What It Is and What It Is Not.* Independently Published: 1859.

Ogden, Pat, Kekuni Minton, and Clare Pain. *Trauma and the Body.* New York: W. W. Norton & Company, 2006.

Poston, Carol, and Karen Lison. *Reclaiming Our Lives.* New York: Bantam Books, 1989.

Phillips, Maggie, and Claire Frederick. *Healing the Divided Self: Clinical and Ericksonian Hypnotherapy for Post-Traumatic and Dissociative Conditions.* New York: W. W. Norton Company, 1995.

Ratner, Ellen. *The Other Side of the Family.* Deerfield Beach, FL: Health Communications, 1990.

Robb, Christina. *Drawing Out the Pain.* Boston Globe, May 14, 1990.

Rogers, Natalie. *The Creative Connection: Expressive Arts as Healing.* Palo Alto, CA: Science and Behavior Books, Inc., 1993.

Rush, Florence. *The Best Kept Secret: Sexual Abuse of Children.* New York: McGraw Hill Publishing, 1980.

Russel, Diana E. H. *The Secret Trauma: Incest in the Lives of Girls and Women.* New York: Basic Books, Inc., 1986.

Samuels, M.D., Michael, and Mary Rockwood Lane, R.N. *Creative Healing: How to Heal Yourself by Tapping Your Hidden Creativity.* Eugene, OR: Resource Publications, 1998.

Samuels, M.D., Michael, and Mary Rockwood Lane, R.N. *Healing with the Arts.* New York: Atria Paperback, 2013.

Scaer, M.D., Robert C. *The Body Bears the Burden.* New York: The Haworth Medical Press, 2001.

Schwartz, Judith S. *Confrontational Clay: The Artist as Social Critic,* Kansas City, MO, Mid-America Arts Alliance, 2000.

Schwartz-Kinney, Beth M., Michelle McCauley, and Michelle A. Epstein. *Child Abuse: A Global View.* Westport: Greenwood Press, 2001.

Shone, Ronald. *Creative Visualization.* Rochester, VT: Destiny Books, 1988.

Spencer, Ph.D., Linda Bushell. *Healing Abuse and Trauma Through Art.* Springfield, IL: Charles C. Thomas, Publisher Ltd., 1997.

Stern, Jessica. *Denial: A Memoir.* New York: HarperCollins Publishers, 2011.

Stone, Ph.D., Hal, and Sidra L. Stone, Ph.D. *Embracing Our Selves.* Novato, CA: New World Library, 1989.

Trepper, Terry S., and Mary Jo Barrett. *Treating Incest: A Mulitple Systems Perspective.* New York: The Haworth Press, 1986.

Tucci, Giuseppe, *The Theory and Practice of the Mandala,* London: Rider & Company, 1969.

Turner, Janine. *Home Is Where the Hurt Is.* Wellingborough, Northamptonshire: Thorsons Publishers Limited, 1989.

Utain, Marsha, and Barbara Oliver. *Scream Louder.* Deerfield Beach, FL: Health Communications, Inc., 1989.

van der Kolk, M.D., Bessel. *The Body Keeps the Score.* New York: Penguin Books, 2014.

Von Blum, Paul. *The Art of Social Conscience.* New York: Universe Books, 1976.

W., Nancy, *On the Path.* San Francisco: Harper Collins Publishers, 1991.

Walker, Alice. *The Color Purple.* New York: Harcourt Brace Jovanovich, 1982.

Ward, Elizabeth. *Father Daughter Rape.* London: The Women's Press Limited, 1984.

Wardell, PhD., RN, Dianne, Sue Kagel, BSN, RN, and Lisa Anselme, BLS, RN. *Healing Touch: Enhancing Life through Energy Therapy,* Bloomington: iUniverse, 2014.

Wisechild, Louise M. *The Obsidian Mirror: An Adult Healing from Incest.* Seattle: The Seal Press, 1988.

Wisechild, Louise M. *She Who Was Lost Is Remembered: Healing from Incest through Creativity.* Seattle: The Seal Press, 1991.

Wolf, Linda Star. *Shamanic Breath Work: Journeying beyond the Limits of the Self.* Rochester, VT: Bear & Company, 2009.

Wood, MA, Wendy, and Leslie Hatton. *Triumph over Darkness: Understanding and Healing the Trauma of Childhood Sexual Abuse.* Kingsport, TN: Arcata Graphics, 1989.

Woodman, Marion. *Addiction to Perfection.* Toronto: Inner City Books, 1982.

Zagon, Laurie. *Art for Healing: Painting Your Heart Out.* Bloomington, IL: AuthorHouse, 2008.

VIDEOS

Litteral, Linda. *My Body in Space and Time,* Nikki Dunnan and Linda Litteral, Art
    Produce, 2021. https://youtu.be/agwPWMZd1Kw

Litteral, Linda. *Wind Whispers,* Mojaveland installation, 2021.
    https://youtu.be/MudjAL73AxI

Meyers, Ted. *Artist Interview Linda Litteral,* Desert Dairy Artist Residency, 2021.
    https://www.youtube.com/watch?v=TyJW69LcgyI

Meyers, Ted. *The Walk: A Project by Linda Litteral,* Feminist Image Group (FIG), Desert
    Dairy Artist Residency, 2021.
    https://www.youtube.com/watch?v=Ycb2QE9QRzA&t=35s

Spiegal, Michaela. *Interview with Linda Litteral,* Centre Pompadour, 2018.
    https://www.youtube.com/watch?v=6MDignAR0oQ&t=10s

Spiegal, Michaela. *Interview with Linda Litteral,* Centre Pompadour, 2018.
    https://www.youtube.com/watch?v=4mXwDfIRe3s

Made in the USA
Las Vegas, NV
07 March 2023